If Teacups Could Talk

SHARING A CUP OF KINDNESS
WITH TREASURED FRIENDS

NARRATIVE BY

Emilie Barnes

PAINTINGS BY

Sandy Lynam Clough

HARVEST HOUSE PUBLISHERS
Eugene, Oregon 97402

Quote on page 19 is taken from Gail Greco, *Tea Time at the Inn.* Rutledge Hill Press, Nashville, TN.

Quote on page 38 by Barbara Rosenthal is taken from Gail Greco, *Tea Time at the Inn,* Rutledge Hill Press, Nashville, TN.

Quote on page 46 by Carol and Malcolm Cohen is taken from *Tea Time at the Inn,* Rutledge Hill Press, Nashville, TN.

Quote on page 66 is taken from Tom Hegg, *A Cup of Christmas Tea.*

Information regarding art prints featured in this book:

Sandy Clough Studios
25 Trail Road,
Marietta, GA 30064

OTHER BOOKS BY EMILIE BARNES

*The Spirit of Loveliness, The Complete Holiday Organizer,
The Creative Home Organizer, Eating Right,
The 15-Minute Organizer, More Hours in My Day,
My Prayer Planner, Survival for Busy Women,
Things Happen When Women Care, 15 Minutes Alone with God,
The 15-Minute Money Manager* and *The Daily Planner*

*To obtain additional information about Emilie Barnes' seminars and tapes
send a self-addressed, stamped business envelope to:*

MORE HOURS IN MY DAY
*2838 Rumsey Drive
Riverside, CA 92506*

Art direction design, and production by
Garborg Design Works, Minneapolis, Minnesota

IF TEACUPS COULD TALK

Copyright © 1994 by Harvest House Publishers
Eugene, Oregon 97402

Library of Congress Cataloging-in-Publication Data

Barnes, Emilie.
    If teacups could talk : sharing a cup of kindness with treasured friends / Emilie Barnes : illustrations by Sandy Lynam Clough
        p.   cm.
        ISBN 1-56507-232-4
        1. Afternoon teas. I. Title
        TX736.B37 1994
        641.5'3—dc20   94-12931
                                                                              CIP

Printed in the United States of America.

    97 98 99 00 01 02 03 04 05 /QH / 16 15 14 13 12 11 10 9 8

To my mama, Irene,
who taught me how to tea…

To our daughter Jenny
and daughter-in-love Maria,
with whom I joy to tea…

To my granddaughter
and those yet to come,
whom I'm teaching how to tea…

And to the special women
with whom I've shared
and will share a cup of tea.

Also to Eileen Mason, my dear friend
and editor at Harvest House,
who caught the vision of this book.

And to my special editor,
Anne Christian Buchanan,
who helped make this book
talk so beautifully.

Contents ~

An Invitation to Tea

—— ✕ ——

If teacups could talk my house would be full of conversation…because my house is full of teacups.

My collection of china cups—begun many years ago, when I set up housekeeping as a child bride—has long since outgrown its home in the glass-front armoire and spread out to occupy side tables and shelves and hooks in the kitchen or to find safe harbor in the dining-room hutch.

Some of these cups I inherited from women I love—my mother and my aunties. Some are gifts from my husband, Bob, or from my children or from special friends. A few are delightful finds from elegant boutiques or dusty antique shops.

One cup bears telltale cracks and scars; it was the only one I could salvage when a shelf slipped and fourteen cups fell in shatters.

Three other cups stand out for their intense color; my aunt was always attracted to that kind of dramatic decoration.

Yet another cup, a gift, is of a style I've never much cared for, but now it makes me smile as I remember the houseguest who "rescued" it from a dark corner of the armoire because it looked "lonely."

Each one of my teacups has a history, and each one is precious to me. I have gladly shared them with guests and told their stories to many people.

Recently, however, I have been more inclined to listen.

I've been wondering what all those cups, with their history and long experience, are trying to say to *me*.

What I hear from them, over and over, is an invitation—one I want to extend to you in this book: *When did you last have a tea party? When was the last time you enjoyed a cup of tea with someone you care about? Isn't it time you did it again?*

Perhaps you have had the privilege of "taking tea" in the grand British style at a distinguished old country inn or a pretty little tea shop. All over the country, people are rediscovering the civilized joys of a traditional afternoon tea, with its elegant settings and its dainty sandwiches, its meticulously arranged platters of luscious sweets and perfectly brewed cups of tea. With a little care and a minimum of expense, you can enjoy this lovely ritual in your own home.

Or perhaps the idea of a tea party takes you back to childhood. Do you remember dressing up and putting on your best manners as you sipped pretend tea out of tiny cups and shared pretend delicacies with your friends, your parents, or your teddy bears? Were you lucky enough to have adults who cared enough to share tea parties with you? And are you lucky enough to have a little person with whom you could share a tea party today? Is there a little girl inside you who longs for a lovely time of childish imagination and "so big" manners?

It could be that the mention of teatime brings quieter memories—cups of

> *"Listen, for I will speak of excellent things,"*
> —THE BOOK OF PROVERBS
> (NKJV)

amber liquid sipped in peaceful solitude on a big old porch, or friendly confidences shared over steaming cups. So many of my own special times of closeness—with my husband, my children, my friends—have begun with putting a kettle on to boil and pulling out a tea tray.

But even if you don't care for tea—if you prefer coffee or cocoa or lemonade or ice water, or if you like chunky mugs better than gleaming silver or delicate china, or if you find the idea of a traditional tea overly formal and a bit intimidating—there's still room for you at the tea table, and I think you would love it there! I have shared tea with so many people—from business executives to book-club ladies to five-year-old boys. And I have found that few can resist a tea party when it is served with the right spirit.

You see, it's not tea itself that speaks to the soul with such a satisfying message—although I must confess that I adore the warmth and fragrance of a cup of Earl Grey or Red Zinger. And it's not the teacups themselves that bring such a message of beauty and serenity and friendship—although my teacups do bring me much pleasure.

It's not the tea, in other words, that makes teatime special, it's the spirit of the tea party.

It's what happens when women or men or children make a place in their life for the rituals of sharing. It's what happens when we bother with the little extras that feed the soul and nurture the senses and make space for unhurried conversation. And when that happens, it doesn't really matter what fills the cups or holds the liquid.

It really isn't the tea.

It's the spirit of the tea party.

And, it is in that spirit that I hope you will join me.

Come and share a pot of tea,
My home is warm and my friendship's free.

Fill Me with Serenity
ISLANDS OF CALM IN AN OCEAN OF CHAOS

If you really want to, you can grab a quick cup of tea.

You can drive by the fast-food window and collect a foam cup full of hot water with a little plastic lid, a packet of sweetener, and a teabag. Then you can sit there in the drive-through lane (while cars honk behind you), lift the lid, stick in the little gauze bag, and set it in the cup holder to steep while you steer back out into the traffic.

Or if you're in a hurry at home or at the office, you can always heat a mug of water in the microwave. Then you can plunk in your teabag or stir in some spiced-tea mix and carry the whole thing back to your desk to gulp while you work.

You really can do that if you prefer.

But I hope you won't do it.

You see, if you insist on instant, you'll get your tea, but you'll miss one of tea's most beautiful benefits—the blessing of slowing down to enjoy it. You'll be having your tea but losing the opportunity to stake out an island of calm serenity in the chaotic ocean of daily life.

Whether your teatime is simple or elaborate, a solitary moment or a friendly gathering, it can help you make room for stillness in even the most frantic day. As a result, its potential for stress reduction is enormous.

Tea takes time—and that's part of the magic. You can't hurry it without losing something vital. The act of making and drinking tea forces us to slow down—and I truly believe our bodies and spirits are desperate to slow down from the frantic pace our culture sets for us today.

People in our society don't like to wait, but you simply cannot hurry a good pot of tea.

You put on the kettle, then you must wait for the water to boil. And while you're waiting, there are little things to attend to. You rinse out the teapot. You fill the cream pitcher and the sugarbowl and set out the teacups—the prettiest ones you have. You might pick a flower or set a candle in its holder or rummage through the cabinet for a pretty plate. Even if you haven't had time to bake, you open a package of cookies and arrange them on the plate.

No, none of these things is absolutely necessary. You can always go back to microwaving water and fishing your cookie directly from the package. You can drink your tea standing up at the counter or gulp it as you run out the door. But again, you'll be missing the opportunity.

You see, boiling the water in a kettle is part of the ritual. Arranging the tea tray is part of a ritual. Preparing and enjoying tea is a ritual in itself.

I love what my friend Yoli Brogger calls it: "a ceremony of loveliness." And I believe with all my heart that human beings crave ritual and ceremony (and loveliness) in our lives.

When we do things a certain way, the way we have done them in the past, the way others before us have done them, something deep in our spirits is comforted.

Children instinctively know this; that's why they delight in family traditions. Teenagers may rebel against established customs, but they create their own. (Watch a teenager get ready to go out in the evening and you'll know how important ritual is to him or her.) Most of us, as we grow older, also grow to cherish the rituals of our lives.

Another satisfying aspect of a ritual lies in its repetition. We quickly learn what to do; we can almost do it without thinking. So after a time, the ritual performs the valuable function of occupying the body and the senses while freeing the mind and spirit.

Have you ever noticed that your mind seems to work better when your body is occupied with something it's done before—like taking a walk or washing dishes or mowing the lawn? The same thing happens to me when I'm rinsing out a teapot or cutting the crust off little sandwiches or arranging tea things on a tray. The little repetitive actions of preparing and serving tea become a reassuring soil out of which thoughts can grow, and conversations can spring.

There's no hurry about any of this, since you can't go ahead with the tea until the water is boiling. And there's more waiting to do even then, because the tea leaves or teabags must steep in the pot. But while you are waiting for the liquid to turn its fragrant amber, you can carry the tray to a comfortable nook and wait in peace. If you are with friends, this is a wonderful time to reconnect with one another. If you are alone, you can read or think or pray or just "be."

> *There are few hours in my life more agreeable than the hour dedicated to the ceremony known as afternoon tea.*
> —HENRY JAMES

The brewed tea is too hot to gulp, but it will cool. You can simply sit and wait until the boiling liquid settles into comfortable warmth. Maybe you can read yet another page of your book. Or you can politely pass the cream and sugar and cookies or fruit to your friends—more ritual.

Then your cup is ready to enjoy. And somehow, as you sip, your mind continues to settle out of its habitual rush. Your words and your musings slow down and sift deeper. Your relationships— even your relationship with yourself—are granted space for a leisurely stretch.

And the beautiful thing is: All this slowness takes so little time!

Enjoying a cup of tea is not like taking a summer off or going away on a retreat. It's an island of calm you can reasonably visit in the course of your busiest day.

If you have to, you can have a tea break in twenty minutes. Thirty is better, an hour ideal. But no matter how much time you take, you won't catch the calming spirit of the tea party unless you let yourself slow down and enjoy it.

In this sense, I think taking tea is a bit like riding the train. The trip from Southern California to Chicago by passenger rail requires several solid days, and unforeseen delays may stretch the journey even longer. If you worry constantly about "when we're going to get there," you'll be a nervous wreck, but you won't get there any faster.

Yet if you can adjust your jet-age expectations to the rhythm of the rails, taking train travel on its own terms, you begin to discover unexpected pleasures. You can walk freely through the roomy aisles or relax in big, comfortable seats. You can enjoy a meal in the dining car or talk to people in the club car or just sit and watch the scenery.

Once you make the decision to adjust your pace, you can relax and enjoy the journey.

Tea is like that too. You may need to change your mental gears to enjoy it fully. You may need to practice waiting and learning to enjoy the repetitive freedom of the ritual. But once you do, the change of pace will renew your mind and refresh your spirit.

Just for Me • A Solitary Tea

You don't need a lot of people to enjoy a lovely tea party. Taking the time to prepare a lovely tea just for you will calm you down and give you a wonderfully pampered feeling. Why not take a break in a long afternoon to enjoy a quiet cup in a lovely spot? Or if you have the luxury of an evening to yourself, why not prepare tea with fruit and sandwiches around five o'clock and then not worry about dinner? You'll have more time to enjoy the evening, and you'll sleep better because you ate early and light.

Here's a simple menu for a solitary tea that is easy to prepare, healthful, and satisfying.

A Perfect Pot of Tea (see instructions on page 14)
Orange or Apple Slices or a Beautiful Bunch of Grapes
Cream Cheese, Celery & Walnut Sandwiches
Homemade or Store-Bought Cookies

While waiting for the water to boil and the tea to steep, prepare one or more sandwiches and arrange them on a plate with the fruit and cookies. Lay a pretty cloth on a tray or on the table and add a flower or a candle for elegance. Then sit down at the table or carry your tray to a cozy spot. Enjoy!

CREAM CHEESE, CELERY AND WALNUT SANDWICHES

This easy-to-do filling can be made in minutes.

¼ pound cream cheese, room temperature

¼ celery heart, very finely chopped

¼ cup diced walnuts

White or whole-wheat bread

Parsley sprigs (for garnish)

In a small bowl, beat cream cheese until smooth. Mix in celery and walnuts. Make sandwiches with cheese mixture. Trim off crusts of bread and cut sandwiches into rectangles or triangles. Garnish plate with sprigs of parsley.

Although my neighbors are all barbarians,

And you, you are a thousand miles away,

There are always two cups on my table.

TANG DYNASTY (618-906 A.D.)

Fill Me with Friendship

THE ART OF BEING WITH ONE ANOTHER

My granddaughter Christine and I are kindred spirits. We bonded when she was an infant—my first grandbaby. Our relationship has been special ever since, and tea parties have been part of that special relationship.

One Saturday afternoon as we were walking to the mailbox together, ten-year-old Christine said, "Grammy, let's make some scones and have tea."

The next thing I knew, we were in the kitchen whipping up our basic scone recipe. In just a matter of minutes we had popped them in the oven and were setting the table for a simple tea party—just Christine and me.

When the scones were done, we sat down. She poured the tea with practiced ease—we've done this before! We smeared the hot, tasty scones with our favorite jam and whipped topping.

But it's what happened next that made the afternoon so special. Once the tea was poured, we began to talk—about friendships, parents, brothers (she has two), and what she could expect as a preadolescent. I was amazed at her knowledge and maturity. We ended up talking about spiritual matters—about God and the meaning of life.

What a delightful experience for both of us—just two people who love each other sharing our lives over a cup of tea! We were forty-five years apart in age, yet seconds apart in spirit. I'll never forget that wonderful afternoon.

But it was only afterward, as I was carefully washing the china cups and returning them to their homes in my oak armoire, that I realized what had happened that afternoon: Christine had asked for a tea party.

But what she was really asking for was *time with me.* Asking for tea was her way of saying "I need to talk to you."

What is there about a cup of tea that invites shared confidences, that nurtures friendships and brings people together? "Tea and sympathy" have been companions for many long years, almost from the first introduction of this Oriental drink in English-speaking countries. For at least two centuries, "Come for tea" has been just another way of saying, "Come, let's share a bit of our lives together."

The very act of preparing and serving tea encourages conversation. The little spaces in time created by teatime rituals call out to be filled with conversation. Even the tea itself—warm and sweet and comforting—inspires a feeling of relaxation and trust that fosters shared confidences.

Even more important, tea nurtures friendship by inviting us to be present to one another—right now, in the moment.

So much in our culture can be done without really being there—without being mentally and emotionally tuned in to the people around us or the task at hand. We can drive and listen to the radio at the same time. We can eat dinner in front of the television. We can go to entertainment events or even to church and sit side by side without truly connecting with one another.

Some of us feel so assailed by the constant noise and pressure around us that we get in the habit of withdrawing, protecting ourselves, not quite being there. Or we do so much at once that our minds are always somewhere else. Have you ever found yourself nodding to a child and pretending to listen while mentally preparing a grocery list or thinking what you need to do tomorrow?

But there is something about a tea party that gently pulls us in the opposite direction. The tea ritual feels safe, comforting, inviting. Quietly and without threat, it calls us out of ourselves and into relationship.

The very process of preparing and drinking tea asks for our attention, our presence. Handling delicate tea things awakens a kind of carefulness that carries over to the way we treat our companions. (This is one reason I favor fragile porcelain over heavy mugs or paper cups.) And when we offer tea to someone, we are also offering ourselves. We are saying, "For the next few minutes I will listen to you. I will treat you with respect. I will be present for you."

Teatime supports a conversation by giving us something to do when the dialogue lags…or hits an uncomfortable snag. If we don't know what to say, we can always pick up another muffin or freshen our companion's cup or just inhale the aroma of our own cup, and thus negotiate the silences to explore deeper levels of companionship.

The relative formality of a traditional teatime also imposes a kind of gentle control on the confidences we share. Teatime is intimate but not intrusive—a time for tears, perhaps, but not for tantrums. Perhaps that's one reason teatime feels so safe, so nurturing. It fosters civilized friendship, and in this age of brutality and chaos a sense of safety is both rare and comforting.

The relationship-enhancing properties of tea make it a wonderful vehicle for getting to know someone new, for patching up a misunderstanding, for sharing good news or supporting one another in bad times. I have seen lives change over teacups. I have seen new friendships forged and old friendships renewed.

> *Somehow, taking tea together encourages an atmosphere of intimacy when you slip off the timepiece in your mind and cast your fate to a delight of tasty tea, tiny foods, and thoughtful conversation.*
> — Gail Greco

I'll never forget the day I got a call that my longtime friend Sue Boydstun, who now lives in Texas, was in our town for a brief visit. I quickly invited her out to our house for tea, then scurried to make arrangements to serve tea out by our pond. Hastily I mixed some scones and popped them into the oven. While they baked, I filled the tray with cups, teapot, a basket for the scones, jam, clotted cream, a candle, and a vase for the flowers I would pick from the yard. Within half an hour I had a lovely tea table set among the trees, just in time for Sue's arrival.

This all happened in the middle of a very busy day for me—but I was so glad I took the time to renew our friendship over our tea. The hour passed quickly, and then we both returned to our busy lives—uplifted and refreshed from our time together.

I don't remember what my "to do" list said on that busy day. But I'll never forget the smile on my friend's face as we walked to the pond to enjoy our teatime together.

When we take the time to tea, we are creating the kinds of memories that cement lifetime friendships. But we have to make room for the memories, disciplining ourselves to put aside the urgent in favor of the truly important.

My dear friend Yoli is known for her one-on-one teas, especially with women who are hurting. Again and again I have seen her reach for the phone with an invitation to "come for tea—just you and me."

Out comes a hand-painted tin tray from Yoli's unique collection. Out comes a pretty teapot and two china cups and saucers. (Yoli always places a heart-shaped doily between the cup and saucer.) Her tea is ready in moments—very simple yet simply beautiful. And then Yoli is sharing heart-to-heart with her guest, giving the wonderful gift of herself. Whenever I go to tea with Yoli, I know to expect laughter, tears, and a lot of love.

Every Christmas Yoli invites her closest friends, one at a time, for a special Christmas tea. For each of us she brings out her lovely antique china, her beautiful candles and flowers, her fresh-baked scones and wonderful apricot turnovers. We spend the time in her beautifully decorated house talking over the past year, praying together, getting to know each other all over again. It shouldn't come as a surprise that some of these friendships have lasted twenty or thirty years! Yoli says that her Christmas teas also help her maintain perspective during the hectic season. In her words "they keep things quiet and sweet."

If Teacups Could Talk

Marriages, too, can grow stronger and more vital over a tea tray. At least that is my experience; teatime has become a time when my Bob and I nurture our friendship as husband and wife. We are business partners as well as marriage partners, so we spend most of our days together. But even then, we find that it's easy to begin traveling on parallel paths—living together and doing our work without really communicating on a personal level.

So Bob and I have come to treasure our tea breaks, which we take together in the afternoon or evening when it's just the two of us. We sit down together, sip our tea, nibble some sandwiches or fruit, and just relax and talk. But our tea talk is not shoptalk. It's not problem talk—this is not the time when we wrestle over the "issues" in our marriage. Our tea talk is friendship talk, and it reminds us of why we're still together after all these years. (We also find there's nothing like an intimate cup of tea together to make us feel romantic!)

My friend Sheri, who does my typing for me, has found that tea parties are a wonderful way of staying close to her daughter. "We do tea parties all the time," she tells me. "Every Christmas morning we get up and have a tea party together before everybody else is up. We also have tea parties on the first day of school and anytime when we're not connecting. I light a candle, arrange a centerpiece, and pull out something I've baked. And then we have a wonderful time together."

I asked Sheri what kind of tea she likes best. "Oh, I'm not a tea drinker," she replied. "I like coffee. I have all my tea parties with coffee."

That's so important to remember!

I love tea, but there's nothing magic about that particular liquid. Tea is not a truth serum or an elixir of love. There is nothing in a cup of tea that cannot be found in a cup of coffee or even in a cup of cold water served with the right attitude.

And people being what they are, it's certainly possible to turn teatime into an occasion for gossip and slander instead of comfort and understanding—a time that hurts relationships instead of nurturing them. "Tea and scandal" is as old a phrase as "tea and sympathy."

It's even possible to sip tea with someone while watching a basketball game on TV or thinking about tomorrow's responsibilities—but why would you want to?

It's not the tea, remember; it's the spirit of the tea party. And the spirit of the tea party is, above all, the spirit of true friendship.

That's why I want to treat my teatime companions—strangers, friends, or family—with the same gentleness and respect I reserve for my delicate china teacups. That's why I want to share myself along with my cookies and crumpets…to sweeten my teatimes with trust and affection.

That's why I want to be fully present—in heart, soul, and mind—to enjoy the sweet communion of kindred spirits over a cup of tea.

Cream Tea for Two • **A One-on-One Party with a Special Friend**

Scones are the staple delicacy of an English tea. Simple and delicious, they resemble a giant, flaky, slightly sweet biscuit. In England they are pronounced to rhyme with *lawn* not *cone*—but however you say the word, scones are wonderful!

In England, a cream tea is one in which the traditional scones are served with clotted cream or Devonshire cream instead of butter. You cannot find the same kind of cream in the United States, our cows and our milk delivery system are different, but there are many possible substitutes. So why not invite a special friend over to enjoy a special one-on-one cream tea with you? This would be a great way to celebrate a birthday or to say thank you.

The key to making this one-on-one tea memorable is to plan and prepare for it just as carefully as you would a tea party for ten. Write out an invitation on a pretty card and send it to your friend, and allow plenty of time to decorate your table and prepare the food.

Tangerine Special Tea
Scones with Butter
Strawberry Preserves, Homemade or Otherwise
Clotted Cream

Buy or pick out two "companion" flowers—two roses, two carnations, two daffodils—and arrange in a vase with ferns or baby's breath. Spread a lovely tea cloth on a table or a tray, and use the very nicest pot and cups you have. Light a candle and set a little gift (a card, a book, a tape, a small decorative object, something you've made) at your friend's place. Put on his or her favorite kind of music. Dress up. Let your time together feel out of the ordinary without being stiff. And use this time to say the kinds of things you may not have shared before—just how much your special friend means to you.

TANGERINE SPECIAL TEA

4 tangerine slices

12 whole cloves

4 sticks of cinnamon

2 tablespoons sugar

4 cups orange pekoe tea brewed with the rind of one tangerine

Stud each slice of tangerine with 3 cloves. Now place a tangerine slice, a cinnamon stick, and 1½ teaspoons sugar in each cup. Fill with hot tea from the pot. Serve, using the cinnamon stick to stir the tea. Recipe makes 4 cups—plenty for two people.

BASIC SCONES

Scones are quite simple to make, so I usually make my own. However, a packaged scone mix can also give you very good results. You can add all kinds of extras to scones, depending on your taste. Try cut-up apples, currants, ginger, orange, almond flavoring, cinnamon, apricots, fresh blueberries, cranberries, or even chocolate chips.

2 cups flour

1 tablespoon baking powder

2 tablespoons sugar

½ teaspoon salt

6 tablespoons butter

½ cup buttermilk

Lightly beaten egg

Mix dry ingredients. Cut in 6 tablespoons butter until mixture resembles coarse cornmeal. Make a well in the center and pour in buttermilk. If you don't have buttermilk, use regular milk. Mix until dough clings together and is a bit sticky—do not overmix. Turn out dough onto a floured surface and shape into a 6-to 8-inch round about 1½ inches thick. Quickly cut into pie wedges or use a large round biscuit cutter to cut circles. The secret of tender scones is a minimum of handling. Place on ungreased cookie sheet, being sure the sides of scones don't touch each other. Brush with egg for a shiny, beautiful brown scone. Bake at 425° for 10 to 20 minutes, or until light brown.

CLOTTED CREAM

Either of these two recipes makes an acceptable substitute for English clotted cream. In a pinch, you can also use commercial whipped topping.

SUE'S CREME FRAICHE

1 cup heavy cream

1 tablespoon buttermilk

Combine the cream and buttermilk in a saucepan over medium heat. Heat just until the chill is off—to about 90°. Pour into a glass jar, cover lightly with a piece of waxed paper, and let set in a warm place (65-70°) for 12 to 20 hours, until thickened. Replace the waxed paper with plastic wrap or a tight-fitting lid and refrigerate for at least 6 hours. (It will keep about two weeks in the refrigerator.) You can whip this substance to make it thicker or add a little sugar if you like your cream sweet.

MOCK DEVONSHIRE CREAM

½ cup heavy cream or 8 ounces softened cream cheese

2 tablespoons confectioners' sugar

½ cup sour cream

In a chilled bowl, beat cream until medium-stiff peaks form, adding sugar during the last few minutes of beating. (If you are using cream cheese, just stir together with sugar.) Fold in sour cream and blend. Makes 1½ cups.

*What part of confidante has that poor teapot played ever
since the kindly plant was introduced among us. Why
myriads of women have cried over it, to be sure! What
sickbeds it has smoked by! What fevered lips have received
refreshment from it! Nature meant very kindly...when she
made the tea plant; and with a little thought, what series
of pictures and groups the fancy may conjure up and
assemble round the teapot and cup.*

WILLIAM MAKEPEACE THACKERAY

Fill Me with Tradition

A SHORT HISTORY OF TEA AND SYMPATHY

Tea was a tradition in my family when I was growing up. My mother and her sisters (my aunts) treasured their beautiful teapots and teacups and delighted in sharing teatime with others. Because my family is Jewish, we enjoyed our tea in the tradition of Eastern European Jews. But as I grew older, I was delighted to find that tea is a tradition that encompasses many cultures and many centuries.

My first experience of afternoon tea in the traditional British style came during a trip to Canada, when Bob and I visited the beautiful Empress Hotel in Victoria, British Columbia—one of the most beautiful old hotels I have ever seen. I was enchanted by the lovely teatime we enjoyed there, and I sought to learn more about this delightful and soul-satisfying custom. The more I learned, the more interested I became. Now I enjoy my tea with fuller appreciation for the many centuries of tradition behind it.

Legend credits the Chinese Emperor Shen Nung (28th century B.C.) with the discovery of tea. Health-conscious even in that early time, the emperor observed that boiling water before drinking seemed to protect people from disease. He always insisted on having his water boiled, and that simple precaution led to a wonderful revelation.

One day while touring the provinces, the emperor stopped for a rest with his entourage. Servants gathered branches from a nearby evergreen bush to build a fire for boiling the emperor's water. A passing wind blew some leaves from the bush into the boiling pot, and soon a delightful aroma issued forth. Intrigued, the emperor drank some of the broth. He immediately declared that the refreshing brew must have medicinal qualities and ordered his servants to gather leaves from the bush to take back to the palace.

News of the emperor's discovery spread quickly throughout the land. Soon everyone in China was drinking tea, and the infusion of that evergreen plant quickly became an important part of the Chinese culture. Gradually, over the centuries, the knowledge and appreciation of tea spread to other parts of the Orient, then traveled West with Portuguese and Dutch traders.

Tea first reached English shores about 1660, and soon tea was flowing everywhere on the island. It was served first in public coffeehouses and in outdoor "tea gardens," then increasingly in homes.

Tea also enjoyed immense popularity in the American Colonies until the late eighteenth century. But when King George III decided to use tea as a source of revenue and raise the import tax on tea sent to the Colonies, the independent-minded Americans rebelled.

The Boston Tea Party of 1773, when colonists dressed as Indians dumped a shipload of tea into Boston Harbor, was one of the events that propelled the Colonies toward independence, and probably led to a marked preference for coffee in the United States.

Anna, the seventh Duchess of Bedford (1783-1857) is credited with originating afternoon tea in England. That charming custom grew out of very practical

> *I like to…think about the houses and the drawing rooms, the kitchens and the cupboards where [the teacups] were kept. And the people who cared for them and what they thought and felt and loved and lost. For as a wise French writer once said, "The reconstitution of the past is a delicate pleasure of which one should not be deprived.*
> —Geraldene Holt

necessity. In those days in England people ate a heavy breakfast, a late dinner, and very little in between. Toward midafternoon the Duchess routinely experienced a "sinking feeling," which she remedied by dining in her boudoir on tea, cakes, tarts, and biscuits at about four in the afternoon.

Soon others followed the Duchess' lead, and in just a few decades the custom of "taking tea" in the afternoon had become well established. At first the practice was limited to the upper classes, but it eventually became so popular that tea shops and tea-rooms began opening for the enjoyment of the general public.

Your Choice of Tea

Tea is made from an evergreen shrub called camellia sinensis, a relative of the flowering camellia that grows best in tropical or subtropical climates. More than three thousand varieties of tea come from this one plant; the differences lie with the region where the tea is grown (climate, soil, and altitude can all affect flavor) and from the way the leaves are processed. Processed teas fall into three different categories: black, green, and oolong.

__Black teas__ are made from leaves that are allowed to "ferment" or oxidize, then are "fired" or heated to remove most of the moisture. The heat is what turns the leaves black. Black teas produce a hearty brew that is higher in caffeine content than other teas (but still lower in caffeine than coffee).

__Green teas__ are not fermented. Instead, the leaves are steamed in large vats before being fired. Green teas are delicate in flavor, light in color, low in caffeine, and very soothing—good for settling the stomach. They are usually enjoyed without sugar, cream, or lemon.

__Oolong teas__ are produced by a relatively new process—partially fermented with a taste that is stronger than green tea, more delicate than black tea.

You'll find teas by many names; most are blends of teas from different areas.

- *Earl Grey* is a popular blend of black tea scented with oil from a small citrus fruit grown in the Mediterranean region. It is a full-bodied tea, good with milk or cream.
- *English breakfast blend* is a combination of teas from India and Ceylon. It too is quite full-bodied and, as the name implies, is often used as a breakfast tea.
- *Lapsang Souchon*, from the Fukian province of China, has a distinctive smoky flavor.
- *Gunpowder* tea is a green tea which is called "pearl tea" in China.
- *Darjeeling* is a rich-tasting black tea from a mountainous region of India. *Assam* is another well-known India tea.
- *Formosa oolong* is quite expensive. It produces a pale liquid with a "peachy" flavor.
- *Orange pekoe* refers to quality, not taste; it is tea made from the whole leaf. (The word *orange* refers to the Dutch House of Orange and was used by Dutch traders to imply nobility.) However, the term is often misused on tea labels to imply flavor.

Herbal teas are actually not teas at all, but "infusions" from the leaves, roots, seeds, or fruits of various plants such as peppermint, jasmine, or chamomile. Herb teas are usually decaffeinated, and some have medicinal uses.

Begin to investigate the many varieties of tea offered—from strong black teas to gentle herbal teas. Whatever you choose, make time for tea to happen today.

By the turn of the century, teatime had acquired its own formal etiquette. Tea services were silver or china. Fine linens were used for tea cloths and serviettes. Tea gowns

The Well-Dressed Tea Table

"A teapot and a few cups are all you need to brew a good pot of tea. But if you're interested in preparing a fancy afternoon tea for guests, you'll probably want to include a few elegant accessories that can turn the simple act of drinking tea into a lovely and refined social gathering….

"A small, yet elegant tea table should be covered with a lace or fine cotton tea cloth. Each teacup and saucer, separated only by a small napkin, may be placed on top of the tea plate. There should be enough room left over on the table for a silver or dark wood tea tray…. On the tea tray should be an elegant teapot, sugar bowl and creamer, a small pot for hot water, and a "slop" bowl, into which guests can pour their last few sips of cold tea before receiving a refill. A covered muffin dish should hold freshly hot muffins, scones, sweet breads or toast. Fresh preserves in a jam dish are also a must. The real *aficionado* will also provide a muffineer—similar in shape to a salt shaker—which guests may use to sprinkle cinnamon, sugar, or brown sugar on their cakes.

"If you wish to brew your tea in front of your guests, a tea caddy or canister should be on hand, complete with a caddy spoon with which to scoop the leaves into the pot…. Even if your teapot has a strainer built into its spout, it's also wise to have a tea strainer through which to pour each cup…. Mote spoons, which guests can use to remove any leaves that may have eluded the filter and strainer, are generally silver and have holes in the bowl. This allows the tea, but not the leaves, to drain back into the cup."

—**John Beilenson**, from *The Book of Tea*

were loose and flowing, with matching hats and gloves. The tea itself was from India or Ceylon (now Sri Lanka), parts of the British Empire. For those who did not favor tea, punch was sometimes served— or coffee and cocoa. And with the tea came decorated platters of dainty sandwiches, scones with berry jam or clotted cream, toast with cinnamon, and other delicacies that have come to be known as "tea food." In working class homes, afternoon tea became a much heartier affair, with cold meats, cheeses, and breads. This evening meal was called "high tea" and often replaced dinner altogether.

The United States can claim two distinct contributions when it comes to tea, both dating from the early twentieth century.

In 1904, visitors to the Louisiana Purchase Exposition in St. Louis sweltered in a heat wave and shunned the hot brew offered by Indian tea growers. An Englishman named Richard Blechynden, who represented the tea growers, tried pouring the tea over ice in order to entice fair visitors. The result was iced tea, which now accounts for 80 percent of the tea drunk in the United States.

The teabag began as the brainstorm of an American tea merchant named Thomas Sullivan, who hit on the idea of providing samples to his customers in small silk pouches. Sullivan's customers soon discovered that the pouches could be put directly (and conveniently) in teapots, and soon orders were pouring in for tea packaged in "those little bags." Before long, teabags had became a widely accepted means of packaging tea.

And now…nearly five thousand years have gone by since Emperor Shen Nung sipped the first cup of tea on that Chinese roadside.

Almost two centuries have elapsed since the Dutchess of Bedford first thought of tea and cakes to carry her through until dinnertime. And quite a few decades have passed since I first saw Mama pour a cup of tea with her sisters, since I received my first china cup as a wedding present, since Bob and I enjoyed that first afternoon tea at the Empress Hotel….

So much time—yet some things do grow better with age. I enjoy my tea now with a sense of history, a sense of kinship with those who have gone before me. And somehow the brew seems all the richer.

If my teacups could talk, after all these years, what wonderful things they could tell me about what has gone before!

What Time Is Tea?

The hour…can be anywhere between three and six o'clock in the afternoon. The general rule is that the earlier tea is served, the lighter the refreshments. At three, tea is usually a snack—dainty finger sandwiches, petits fours, fresh strawberries; at six, it can be a meal—or "high" tea—with sausage rolls, salads, and trifle. You can serve high tea around the dining room table, but afternoon tea is more of a living room occasion, with everything brought in on a tray or cart.

—**Angela Hynes**, *The Pleasures of Afternoon Tea*

The Proper Way · A Traditional Victorian Afternoon Tea

Not all your tea parties have to follow the guidelines of traditional etiquette, but I urge you to try a traditional afternoon tea at least once. In my experience, those who sample a traditional Victorian afternoon tea find it absolutely delightful!

Begin your planning with an invitation. In Victorian days the invitations were beautifully engraved on white paper. Today almost anything goes—even a phone call. But there is something about a written invitation that honors a guest—as well as providing her with a written reminder of the date and time of the occasion. Printed invitations on lovely white paper are still a lovely touch for a tea party. A printed border of roses or pansies is also appropriate, and so are "teacup" note cards.

The wording should be simple and clear:

Emilie Barnes
requests the pleasure
of your company for
afternoon tea.
Saturday, July 9
between three and five o'clock.
R.S.V.P.

> *I think of half-past four at Manderley, and the table drawn before the library fire…the performance, never-varying, of…the silver tray, the kettle, the snowy cloth.*
> —Daphne du Maurier, *Rebecca*

Once the invitations are out, turn your thoughts to preparing the table. Traditional tea parties call for a lovely white cloth of linen, lace, or crisp cotton. In a pinch you can use a clean white sheet and dress it up with white doilies. You will also need white linen or cotton serviettes (napkins) for each person.

The centerpiece is normally a fresh bouquet of roses and greenery, or a bunch of daisies and baby's breath will also do. Don't get hung up on decorations; in a traditional afternoon tea, the food is the real centerpiece. I do love to use a few candles or oil lamps on my tea table to add romance and warmth.

Next, get out all your pretty serving pieces, the ones you never use—Grandma's teapot, teacups, silver tray, other silver pieces, china plates. What if you don't have all these collected and inherited lovelies? Use what you have—even if it is only paper goods—or borrow from friends. The proper "equipment" adds that special touch to a formal afternoon tea, but don't let the lack of it keep you from experiencing the fun of a tea party.

If you enjoy your tea, you can then begin collecting the proper accoutrements. Over the years, in addition to all my teacups, I have collected special dishes, silver teapots, lovely trays, and crisp linens for my tea parties. Many were forgotten treasures I uncovered at garage or estate sales. When one of my aunts died, I inherited many of her pretty things that are perfect for my tea parties.

Look in antique shops or thrift shops for china, silver, and linen. Let friends and family know you'd love "tea things" for birthdays or Christmas—a single silver spoon, dainty tongs for serving lumps of sugar, a bone-china teacup or teapot, a damask linen cloth. These are heirlooms you will one day pass down to the next generation. They will also motivate you to have more tea parties!

A Timetable for Preparation

ONE WEEK AHEAD
- Order fresh flowers or plan centerpiece.
- Select and prepare linens (launder, iron, or send out).
- Select music.
- Plan menu. (Make sure you know where you can buy all the necessary ingredients.)

TWO DAYS AHEAD
- Shop for ingredients.
- Prepare any recipes you can freeze.
- Don't forget candles, doilies, and sugar cubes.

ONE DAY BEFORE TEA
- Wash and dry teapots, teacups, plates, and trays.
- Polish silver.
- Set table with cloth, teapots, and teacups.
- Make any sandwiches that can be wrapped in plastic and kept in refrigerator.

MORNING OF THE TEA
- Finish setting table with silverware and silver or glass pieces.
- Pick up fresh flowers or pick garden flowers.
- Arrange centerpiece and set candles in place.
- Make and bake last-minute-type recipes.
- Wash and pat dry any garnish you'll be using (such as parsley or mint).
- Slice lemons and cover with plastic wrap.
- Be sure you have enough serviettes for each guest.
- Fill teakettle with water ready to heat.

ONE HOUR PRIOR TO TEATIME
- Mix and cut scones; have ready to pop into oven.
- Place cakes and similar foods on the tea table.
- Pour cream (milk) into small pitcher.
- Fill sugarbowl with sugar cubes.
- Get dressed.
- Put refrigerated items on table.
- Check the table—have you forgotten anything?
- Spray potpourri around room. (Don't let it fall on the food!)
- Greet guests with a warm smile as they arrive.
  —**John Beilenson**, from *The Book of Tea*

Once your table is arranged and your guests have arrived, you'll want to serve your tea in the proper way.

The cream goes first into the cups. Yes, the English use cream in their tea, although it's really milk. The tannins in strong black tea will cause real cream to curdle, so milk is used but called cream. The sugar—in cube form only, please—goes in next.

Of course, you will ask your guests ahead of time whether they want cream or sugar. Some will ask for two lumps, and children may ask for as many as six! The sugar cubes go into the cups and then, finally, the brewed tea. Be sure to pour the tea slowly; fill the cup but don't pour in so much as to cause a spill. A silver teaspoon, usually a tiny one, is used to stir the tea. I use my children's silver-plated baby spoons for stirring; these make wonderful conversation pieces.

For guests who don't care for tea but still want to join the teatime festivities, consider serving punch in a beautiful cut-glass bowl. This is a long-standing English tradition.

Our menu for afternoon tea will be a traditional array of tender scones, dainty tea sandwiches, and luscious sweets:

Darjeeling or Assam Tea
Scones with Clotted Cream and Lemon Curd
Tea Sandwiches
Trifle Fit for a Queen
Emilie's Triple Chocolate Fudge Cake

LEMON CURD

Lemon curd, sometimes called lemon cheese, is a very common English preserve. It is used as a spread for sandwiches, muffins, crumpets and so forth, and it also makes a delicious tart filling.

Grated peel of 4 lemons
Juice of 4 lemons (about 1 cup)
4 eggs, beaten
½ cup butter, cut in small pieces
2 cups sugar

In the top of a large double boiler, combine lemon peel, lemon juice, eggs, butter, and sugar. Place over simmering water and stir until sugar is dissolved. Continue to cook, stirring occasionally, until thickened and smooth. While hot, pour into hot, sterilized ½-pint canning jars, leaving about an ⅛ inch for headspace. Run a narrow spatula down between lemon curd and side of jar to release air. Top with sterilized lids; firmly screw on bands. Place in a draft-free area to cool and store in a cool, dry place. (I keep in the refrigerator.) Lemon curd doesn't keep indefinitely, so make only as much as you will use in a couple of weeks. Makes about 1 pint.

TEA SANDWICHES

Afternoon tea sandwiches are made from very thinly sliced bread with crusts removed. Spread bread with unsalted butter, herb butter, mayonnaise, or cream cheese. Add filling and cut into squares, rectangles, or diamond shapes—or use cookie cutters for round or heart-shaped sandwiches. Tea sandwiches may be made ahead, covered with a damp tea towel or plastic wrap, and refrigerated until serving time. Decorate serving trays with fresh flowers or herbs.

CUCUMBER SANDWICHES are perhaps most commonly associated with afternoon tea. Peel cucumbers and slice very thin. Sprinkle slices with salt and drain on paper towels. Spread white bread with unsalted butter and a thin layer of cream cheese and layer cucumbers no more than ¼ inch high. Cut into desired shapes.

WATERCRESS SANDWICHES are also favorite tea-party fare. Butter white or rye bread and fill with watercress leaves. Cut into squares, arrange on plate, and garnish with watercress.

OTHER TEA SANDWICH IDEAS:
• Thinly sliced chicken breast or smoked salmon with watercress and mayonnaise on white bread.
• Bagel rounds (slice one bagel in thirds horizontally). Spread with cream cheese and topped with thin slices of smoked salmon, tomato rounds, minced onions, and capers.
• Stilton cheese crumbled over apple slices on pumpernickel bread.
• Cream cheese mixed with chutney, a dash of curry, and lemon juice on white bread.
• Paper-thin slices of red radish on white bread spread with unsalted butter.

• Tomato slices sprinkled with freshly chopped basil on rye bread spread with mayonnaise.

TRIFLE FIT FOR A QUEEN
Trifle is a wonderful English dish, perfect for tea!

5 peaches, peeled and sliced
⅔ cup plus 2 tablespoons peach schnapps
One 5 x 9 inch pound cake, purchased or homemade
Fresh berries for garnish
10 ladyfingers
1 recipe Peach Cream (recipe follows)
1 cup whipping cream
2 tablespoons sugar

Brush flat sides of ladyfingers with ⅓ cup of peach schnapps and line the sides and bottom of a glass serving bowl with 8 to 10 cup capacity. Spoon half of the Peach Cream over the ladyfingers lining the bottom of the dish. Arrange half of the peaches on top of the Peach Cream. Slice cake lengthwise into ½ inch slices and brush cake slices on both sides with ⅓ cup schnapps. Arrange half of the cake slices on top of peaches. Repeat layers of Peach Cream, peaches, and cake slices. Whip cream until me-dium soft peaks form. Add sugar and 2 table-spoons schnapps and continue beat-ing until blended. Spread cream mix-ture over the top of trifle and garnish with fresh berries. Wrap tightly with plastic wrap and refrigerate overnight. Makes 8 servings.

PEACH CREAM
8 egg yolks
2¼ cups half-and-half

3 tablespoons peach schnapps
6 tablespoons sugar
4 teaspoons cornstarch

In a medium bowl beat egg yolks until thickened. Gradually add sugar and beat until mixture is thick and lemon colored. Pour into a saucepan and beat in 2 cups half-and-half. Mix cornstarch with remaining half-and-half and beat into egg mixture. Cook over medium-low heat and stir con-stantly until mixture thickens (6 to 8 minutes). Do not let mixture boil. Remove from heat and stir in the peach schnapps. Cool to room tem-perature and then chill. Mixture will thicken more as it cools.

EMILIE'S TRIPLE CHOCOLATE FUDGE CAKE
This is so easy and so good, a hit with every bite! You may want to have it at every tea party!

1 small package chocolate pudding mix (not instant)
1 box chocolate cake mix (dry mix)
½ cup semisweet chocolate pieces
½ cup chopped nuts
Whipped cream

Cook pudding as directed on package and blend dry cake mix into hot pud-ding. (Mixture will be thick.) Pour into prepared oblong pan (13 x 9½ x 2 inches) and sprinkle with chocolate pieces and nuts. Bake 30 to 35 min-utes at 350°. Cool 5 minutes, cut into 2-inch squares, and arrange on cake plate or doily-lined tray. Serve plain or topped with a dollop of whipped cream.

Yea, I have a goodly heritage.

THE BOOK OF PSALMS

Fill Me with Memories

THE LEGACY OF THE TEACUP

I can see it clearly if I close my eyes.

There is the little room with the sofa and chair, the table, the little cabinet. We live there, and at night, when the Murphy bed folds down from the wall, we sleep there too. There are the doors opening onto the tiny kitchen and the minuscule bathroom, and there is the curtain that separates our living quarters from the dress shop.

It's a simple place, even shabby—no designer fabric on the furniture, no decorator carpet on the floor, nothing glamorous or luxurious or expensive.

And yet there on the stove a kettle has just finished singing and is still whistling a little under its breath. Mama's teapot is full and warm, and her English china cups sit expectantly beside it. A little bouquet of flowers sprouts from a vase, and the glow of a candle turns everything golden.

There is Mama, reaching to pour the tea.

There is our guest, one of Mama's customers, smiling and saying, "Just sugar, thank you—no cream."

There I am, having tea with them.

And I am smiling too.

What a wonderful place tea occupies in my memory—even during those very difficult times in my life! When I was just eleven, after my alcoholic father died, my mother moved us into those three little rooms behind her little dress shop. Mama had to work long hours to provide for my brother and me. She designed and sold dresses, took care of alterations, and often worked far into the night doing the books. (Even at that young age, I took over most of the housework.)

And yet, in spite of it all, Mama always managed to have time for a tea party. She would invite a guest—a friend or a neighbor or a customer— through the little curtain that served as our front door. Then it would be time to put on the kettle, warm up the teapot, look for some cookies, and carefully lift the cups from their place of honor in the cabinet. Before I knew it, we would be having a party.

And Mama kept on having tea parties long after I grew up and married and moved away. She lost her business when she was 66 and had to move in with us. When we went to pick her up, she had only two suitcases and a little box of personal belongings, but her two English bone-china cups were carefully packed in the top of that box.

A few years later Mama moved herself and her teacups to an efficiency apartment in a senior-citizen building. Now she lived in a single room—with a bed, a chest of drawers, a small round table, a sofa, a chair, a hot plate, and a tiny bathroom. But Mama's neighbors on the fourteenth floor soon learned to appreciate that little Jewish woman and her tea parties.

Every afternoon Mama would light a candle and put the kettle on the hot plate. She would arrange a small dish of cookies, strudel, or banana bread and stick a pansy or a dandelion or a sprig of ivy in a vase. She would get out her teapot and teacups and open her door a couple of feet—a signal to the neighbors that it was time to come and "sip tea with Irene." Then she would wait for someone to share tea with her...and someone always came.

One afternoon Mama felt a little weary, so she thought she would have a rest before putting on the kettle. She went to her bed and laid her head on the pillow. Then she quietly changed her address from earth to heaven...while her two beautiful English china teacups sat expectantly on the table.

Mama's teacups belong to me now, and I treasure them. But my mother left me so much more than the cups—and I am just now coming to understand the richness of my heritage. As I look back on her life and mine, I can see so clearly what she gave me.

My mother taught me the practical skills of running a home—preparing meals, washing clothes, cleaning toilets (and teapots). A tailor's daughter herself, she passed along her knack for sewing and her love of fine fabrics and beautiful clothes. Later she taught me the basics of business as I worked beside her in the dress shop.

And I learned other lessons from Mama—less tangible, but just as important.

I learned what it means to care for myself and to care for others.

I learned that you have to keep going when life gets hard, but that you don't have to wait until things are perfect to invite others into your life.

I learned from my mother that you can easily turn a kettle and a couple of cups into a full-blown celebration.

Mama left me a wonderful legacy along with her teacups—a legacy of learning and memory. And with it, I believe, she left me a responsibility. It is up to me to pass the legacy of the teacup along to generations that follow.

One Sunday in church, our pastor asked each of us to turn to the person in front of us and ask a question: "Who was the person who most influenced you in your life?"

A beautiful young woman with a thick brown French braid turned around and answered without hesitation, "my grandmother." She then proceeded to tell about how honest her grandmother had been, how she had never said a bad word about anyone. On and on went the compliments about this favorite person in that young woman's life.

I couldn't help but wonder, *Will my grandchildren ever say that about me some-*

day? And I realized anew how important it is to give ourselves to others, especially to those younger than we are, the way my mama gave herself to me and to others.

And what does all this have to do with a tea party? Simply this: Sharing tea with children is just one more tangible way of offering the gift of our time and our attention, sharing ourselves and passing on what we've learned.

One of my favorite tea parties is celebrated each July, a few days after our granddaughter Christine's birthday. That's when she and I and a friend or two plan and enjoy our annual Christine Tea Party. This is a fun party for me, but I don't do it just for the fun. I am very conscious of passing along the legacy of the teacup to this special little girl. At ten years of age, Christine already knows how to prepare the teapot, bake cookies and scones, pick flowers for the centerpiece, set the tea table, and dress up for the party.

The popularity of our annual party is growing. For years we have invited one special friend and her favorite doll. This year Christine invited two friends—and any of their dolls who were old enough to have tea!

Whatever the guest list, we always do the whole preparation for this special occasion. Aprons come on, and the flour flies as the scones are rolled, cut, placed on cookie sheets, and slid into the oven. (Scones are really Christine's favorite to serve because they can be smeared with jam and whipped or clotted cream. But she also loves to make cookies.)

> *It's very important for us to use our best china, silver and linens [when children come to tea]....I've had many children's teas and nothing gets broken. In fact, it's the parents that are watching, worrying that my good china will get broken. I don't worry at all. It never happens.*
>
> —Barbara Rosenthal, Honeysuckle Hill Inn, West Barnstable, Massachusetts

Christine's favorite location for the tea party is the old treehouse that we have renamed the "Cup of Tea House." The girls set the table themselves with the traditional white tea cloth and the snowy cloth serviettes, and of course a white candle. They are so cute as they run through the grounds, picking just the right flowers for the table.

When it's all set, the table looks beautiful sitting high above the ground in that 75-year-old tree. And we are all beginning to feel the excitement as party time draws nearer.

Now the aprons come off. We all troop to Grammy's closet to find just the right dress-up clothes for fine and proper ladies, then to Grammy's powder room, where the makeup flows and the mascara rolls. Dewy eyes and pink rosebud lips are set off by floppy, flowery hats. Gloves and small handbags complete the picture.

Now the time has come for each girl to pick her teacup from my collection. The porcelain and bone-china cups gleam on the glass shelves—some richly colored and trimmed in gold, some very simple, many with rosebuds, a few with birds. All are delicate and shiny clean, but each is unique and different—just as each of the girls is different. Some cups almost seem to smile; others show a painful crack or chip.

It's fun to watch the girls gaze at the cups and try to decide which to use for their tea. At last the choices are made and the cups are placed on the tea tray to be carried carefully outside. Before we go, though, I take a few minutes to talk with the girls about their teacups—and even give a bit of history of the cup of their choice.

"Christine, your teacup was a gift to me from your Aunt Maria on the first Christmas she came into our lives."

"Michelle, your teacup belonged to my auntie, who died last year at 88 years of age. I used to have tea in that cup when I was a little girl and would go to visit her for a week every summer."

"Leah, your teacup was a gift from Papa Bob when we went on a trip to Canada and had tea at the beautiful Empress Hotel in Victoria. That was my first real English tea party, and Papa Bob bought me that cup as a remembrance of that very special time."

There's something else I always tell the girls: "All of our teacups are very delicate and precious to me. We must be careful with them. But if an accident should happen

---

Teatime Collectibles: A Tangible Legacy

Tea can make a fascinating subject for collectors. In addition to collections of teacups like mine, some people collect:

• *Teapots.* Some people specialize in novelty teapots; others like certain kinds of porcelain or silver.

• *Children's tea sets.* These range from minuscule to medium-sized and are made from a wide array of materials.

• *Spoons.* I collect silver baby spoons to stir tea. You could also collect slotted "mote spoons," which were intended to remove any stray leaves from the brew, or just little demitasse spoons.

• *Tea tags* (from teabags). The first tea tag was used by Sir Thomas Lipton in 1917 as an advertising gimmick, and these little items have been produced in a fascinating variety ever since. Some are die-cut in a variety of shapes. Most sport company names, but some carry "did you know" facts, quotable quotes, or even Scripture verses.

• *Tea canisters* (from commercial brands of tea). These come in a dazzling array of shapes and sizes and can make wonderful collectibles.

• *Tea trays.* My friend Yoli has a wonderful collection of hand-painted metal ones.

• *Books about tea*—historical, inspirational, and recipe. Start with this one!

and one should get broken, I want you to remember that you are far more precious to me than any of those teacups! (Besides, Grammy broke some of hers once!)"

The tea party begins as the little girls climb the stairs into the Cup of Tea House. Christine chooses one friend to pour the tea and another to pass the scones. I get the privilege of caring for their "babies," who have been fed and diapered, ready for a nap.

What fun to watch precious children enjoy a tea party like Christine's! I love the thought that I am building memories for them that may last as long as my memories of tea with Mama. But those tea parties are doing so much more.

On one level, I have taught basic skills of hospitality and etiquette that will serve these girls well later in life. They have learned something about planning, baking, preparing tea, decorating a table. They are learning to say please and thank you, to ask before reaching.

They are also learning that worthwhile things in life take a little effort, a little finesse. They are learning that there is value in quiet things, and that these are worth the time and effort that grownups invest in making their tea party happen. They are learning that manners make things easier, not harder, and that it's important to take care of things—but people are more important! Most of all, they are learning that they are part of a long legacy of love, and they will someday be able to pass on that heritage to their children.

I began to see the fruit of all that teaching on the afternoon Christine and I had tea—just the two of us. I watched Christine put her napkin in her lap, ask if she could pour me a cup of tea, say "yes, please" and "no, thank you" and "please pass the jam" and "I'd love to." And it wasn't just "manners." Gradually, through many years of tea parties, Christine had been learning real courtesy, real concern for others.

The legacy of the teacup has been placed in my hand and heart—a gift from my mother and from others who took the time to tea with me. I want to pass it on so the spirit of the tea party will continue long after I am gone. And it is being passed on! My mama's legacy has spread not only to her children and grandchildren, but also to women all over the country who have heard me speak and have caught the spirit of the tea party. They, too, are passing it on; they write to tell me so.

I only wish Mama could know how far her teacups have traveled!

But then again, I think perhaps she does.

> *"I can just imagine myself sitting down at the head of the table and pouring out the tea,"* said Anne, shutting her eyes ecstatically. *"And asking Diana if she takes sugar! I know she doesn't but of course I'll ask her just as if I didn't know."*
> —Lucy Maud Montgomery,
> *Anne of Green Gables*

All Dressed Up •A Grownup Party for Children

Children love to play dress-up, and they love to have tea. So gather a group of your favorite little people for this special party. Children can be anywhere from about four to ten or eleven, but you will have to adjust your activities to the age group. A group of three to five children is a manageable number, or invite children with their parents.

And don't assume that a tea like this is just for girls. Most little boys, in my experience, relish their own special teatimes, and the adults who bother to ask them to tea end up learning a lot about the children and themselves.

Let the children (or the little host or hostess) help with as much of the preparation as possible; older children can do a lot of it themselves. Buy or make some pretty cards for invitations, or let the children make them. (Be sure the basic facts are there—and readable!)

Spend some time before the day of the party hunting up dress-up clothes—hats, scarves, jewelry, gloves, handbags, artificial flowers. You might find that a trip to the thrift shop (or an older relative) yields many treasures for very little money.

Allow at least half an hour before the tea goes on the table for everyone to dress up. (If grownups are part of this party, they should dress up too.)

The menu for this children's party was put together with the help of a child! Children love petits fours—the little cakes are just their size—and you can get them from almost any bakery. If you can't find them and don't want to make them, just serve an assortment of small cookies. The cream-cheese mints are very easy and fun for children to make.

Pink Tea (Pink Lemonade or Strawberry Herbal Tea)
Party Pinwheels or Simple Tea Sandwiches
Strawberries with Confectioners' Sugar for Dipping
Petits Fours or Cookie Assortment
Cream Cheese Mints

PARTY PINWHEELS

1-pound loaf of unsliced day-old white bread (fresh bread will be difficult to cut)
½ cup unsalted butter, room temperature
Filling of your choice. (I like plain cream cheese sprinkled with paprika, but you could also use egg salad, tuna, or any other soft filling—even peanut butter!)

Neatly cut off all crusts from loaf of bread. Lightly spread butter to edges of one long side. Cut lengthwise into as thin a slice as possible. Spread buttered side of slice with filling. Roll up lengthwise, jelly-roll style. Wrap in foil. Repeat until loaf is finished—you should have about 6 rolls. Refrigerate for at least an hour; butter will harden and hold rolls together. Before serving, cut each roll crosswise in about 5 slices. Makes about 30 pinwheels.

CREAM CHEESE MINTS

2¼ cups confectioners' sugar
3 ounces softened cream cheese
Peppermint flavoring to taste (about ¼ teaspoon)
Food coloring
Granulated sugar
Candy molds (optional)

Mash cheese and mix in sugar. If you will be using more than one color, divide mixture and place in separate bowls. Add flavoring and color sparingly; you want soft pastels with a delicate flavor. Stir together until mixture resembles pie dough. Roll into small balls and roll each ball in granulated sugar. Press balls into patties with glass dipped in granulated sugar or press them into candy molds and unmold at once. (Shake sugar into mold, if necessary, to prevent sticking.)

A Teddy Bear Tea • A Child's Party for Grownups

Who doesn't sometimes long to be a child again? Even people who "never had a childhood" may wax nostalgic for the days when imagination ruled and the biggest decision of the day was "What shall I play now?" A teddy bear tea for grownups can be both poignant and enchanting.

If you can, send invitations on teddy-bear stationery; it's very easy to find. Ask guests to bring their favorite teddy bear or stuffed animal from childhood. (If they don't have a bear they should borrow one from their favorite little person.) At some point during the tea, have each guest tell the story of his or her bear.

Decorate the party area with toys (borrow some if you don't have children). If the season is right, pick a big bouquet of wildflowers, including dandelions, and place in a child's water glass. (Don't do this too far in advance; many wildflowers fade quickly). Lullaby tapes (available in children's shops or baby boutiques) provide soothingly appropriate background music. If you have them, serve your tea in demitasse cups or even in tiny children's teacups. Keep the scale as small as possible.

For entertainment at your party, try reading some wonderful children's books aloud—a chapter or two from *Winnie the Pooh* can delight the most serious grownup child. After tea you might even want to play "pin the tail on the donkey,"or you can just reminisce about your own childhoods. Be aware, though, that childhood memories might be painful for some people. If your guests seem reticent, don't probe; just try to make your teatime environment as safe and cozy as possible.

The menu for the teddy bear tea is designed to be simple, comforting, and reminiscent of childhood. Use your choice of ingredients for the sandwiches, but be sure to cut off the crusts, tea party style, and cut the sandwiches into little squares or triangles—however you liked them as a child!

Cinnamon-Apple Tea or Other Fruit Tea
Peanut Butter and Jelly Sandwiches
Oatmeal Cookies
Mama's Cinnamon Bears

MAMA'S CINNAMON BEARS

These bears are based on my mother's wonderful sugar-cookie recipe.

1¾ cups sifted all-purpose flour
½ teaspoon baking powder
½ teaspoon baking soda
½ cup sugar
1 stick butter
1 egg
2 tablespoons milk
1 tablespoon vanilla extract
Sugar and cinnamon for sprinkling

Sift together flour, baking powder, baking soda, and sugar into large bowl. With pastry blender or 2 knives, cut butter into flour mixture until mixture has the consistency of coarse cornmeal. With fork, stir in egg, milk, and vanilla. Mix well with hands to form dough into a ball. Wrap in waxed paper and chill for 2 hours. Preheat oven to 350°. Lightly grease cookie sheets. Divide dough into 4 parts. On lightly floured surface, roll out each part to ⅛ inch thickness. Cut dough with bear-shaped cookie cutters. Bake for 7 minutes, or until golden, and sprinkle with a mixture of sugar and cinnamon. Cool completely. Makes 60 cookies.

I love things that bear the touch of time, chips and all—they're more beautiful than perfection.

BALLERINA QUOTED IN *VICTORIA* MAGAZINE

Fill Me with Courage and Comfort

THE VULNERABLE LESSONS OF PORCELAIN

Collecting teacups in Southern California is really an act of faith.

As I write, the memory is still fresh of a major earthquake not far from where I live. Our home was safely south of the epicenter, and my tea things were safe, but friends and acquaintances have shown me heart-stopping photographs of knee-deep rubble. Days of shaking and aftershocks left all their breakable treasures in shards and shatters.

It wouldn't take much of an earthquake to send all my teacups and teapots crashing to the floor.

Actually, it wouldn't take an earthquake at all, for my fragile teacups are also vulnerable to more mundane dangers—the cat, the feather duster, my grandchildren, my own carelessness.

It's happened before. When children come to tea at my house and go to choose their teacups from my collection, I always have to confess that once I broke fourteen of my own prized teacups! A glass shelf was balanced precariously after cleaning, and it collapsed at my accidental nudge. More than a dozen of my favorite cups fell to smithereens.

The Traveling Tea Party

Here's what to pack for a traveling tea party:

- Large basket with handle
- Tea cloth and serviettes (you can make these your-self from print fabric or sheets)
- 2 teacups and saucers
- 2 tea plates
- 2 dessert forks
- Small dish for butter or other spread
- 2 or 3 small serving plates
- 1 four-cup teapot (if basket is going to a place where hot water is avail-able)
- Thermos bottle (if you are taking your tea on a picnic)
- Tea strainer
- Butter knife
- Two teaspoons
- Tea foods (don't forget butter and spreads)
- Cream, lemon wedges, and lumps of sugar
- Tea
- Candleholder and candle
- Matches
- Small vase and silk flowers
- Several tea towels (use to wrap breakable items)

Pack the tea cloth last, use it to cover the top of the basket.

I was so devastated I couldn't face what happened. I simply swept the china splinters into a box and put in on the shelf, and six years passed before I could muster the courage to look inside the box. Only one cup was in large enough pieces even to be salvaged with glue, and it will never be the same.

All this is to say that I take a significant risk in keeping my teacups out. I take a risk in using them, in letting others use them. But it's a risk I choose to take. I choose it with my eyes open, and I choose it with gladness.

After all, life is fragile, too.

We take a risk just walking out of the door in the morning. We take a risk even if we never cross the threshold.

But if we let that risk stop us from living, we've already lost! While protecting ourselves from injury and loss, we're also cutting ourselves off from joy and growth. And we're not really protecting ourselves at all, since we can never be immune from the inherent dangers of being human and mortal.

I don't want to be foolish. I certainly try to be careful when handling delicate china. I am even looking into ways to secure my cabinets to minimize earthquake damage.

But at the same time, a full and worthwhile life will always call for a certain risk and a certain courage. And my teacups, in all their lovely vulnerability, remind me of that.

The daintiness and yet elegance of a china teacup focuses one to be gentle, to think warmly and to feel close.

—Carol and Malcolm Cohen

There is always a limit to the precautions one can take, and a certain amount of breakage is inevitable. But life in all its vulnerable beauty is incomparably worth it.

It is this realization that has taught me to take risks with my teacups, to avoid the temptation to fall back on "safe" mugs or even paper cups. I've even learned to take those teacups traveling—outdoors on our grounds, on a picnic, or even in a basket to visit a friend. Once I move past the "safety" mentality, I can use my beautiful tea things as they were intended—to share joy and friendship and caring, truly a "cup of kindness."

My friend Marilyn Heavilin told me a wonderful tea-party story about a time when she took her teacups traveling and created a precious and durable memory.

My friend Diana had been through a very rough year. Her husband had had a stroke at the age of 47 which had forced him into retirement. Diana was caring for him as well as working full time at an outside job. She loved to attend the outdoor concerts in the summertime at the Redlands Bowl. We arranged for a night that she could have someone else stay with her husband. We told her we would go early and save seats so she could come as late as she needed to. When she arrived, I opened my picnic basket and we had a tea party. Diana is from England and loves tea and teatime. I had hot tea in a thermos, and I served it in my most delicate china cups. I had bought yummy desserts from a deli…and served them on china plates. I used my best silverware and linen napkins. I also gave Diana a beautiful picture book about English teatime. We had a crowd watching us and drooling!… The setting was perfect, the music was inspiring, the sky was filled with stars, and my friend Diana felt loved and pampered. She will never forget that night, nor will I.

I have had similar experiences many times, and I have never regretted packing up a tea party and taking it to make a memory. Once I took a tea party in a basket to a friend who had been sick. I told her to relax on the couch while I cleared off the coffee table and opened my basket, which contained all the makings of the tea party except the hot water. I put her kettle on to boil while I unpacked a tea cloth and napkins, a candle and a candleholder, a little potted plant (which I left as a gift), and all the other tea things.

Caring for Your Tea Things

The china, silver, and linen you use for tea are worth some risk, but they also deserve loving care. Here are some ideas for preserving your beautiful tea things:

• If you have lace tablecloths that have been stained or yellowed, put a cup of enzyme bleach (such as Biz) in a bucket of water and soak cloth for about three days, then put through wash cycle. Regular bleach can yellow the delicate fabric or cause it to fall apart.

• To clean your silver, try rubbing with toothpaste. Or place aluminum foil in bottom of sink, fill sink with water, and add 1 cup Tide detergent (don't use another kind). Dump in silver pieces and let set for eight to twelve hours, or until tarnish-free.

• If the inside of your china teapot turns brown, clean with bleach. Be sure to rinse thoroughly before using.

• To get the sticky price tag off a new cup or saucer, use nail polish remover.

We enjoyed a delectable teatime together. Then, after tea, I rubbed her feet.

What a wonderful experience for me as well as my friend! That kind of giving and receiving not only makes memories; it forges powerful bonds between people. It minis-

ters health of body and spirit—and that's certainly worth some risk to a china teacup!

There's another lesson I have learned about teacups, but I learned it while watching a program on archaeology. You see, ceramic objects may be breakable, but they are also amazingly resistant to weathering and corrosion and age. Much of what we know about ancient civilizations we have learned from bits of pottery they left behind. China dishes recovered from shipwrecks are often good as new, long after the ship itself has dissolved in the saltwater!

Porcelain is fragile, in other words, but it's also remarkably durable—like us. Like life!

Humans are beautiful and breakable, like china cups…yet we are also strong and resilient. And unlike my cups, humans can heal and grow and move beyond disaster. We can reach out to one another in courage and comfort.

So what will I do when another earthquake comes?

I guess I'll do what anyone must do when disaster strikes:

I'll pick up the pieces.

I'll try to help someone and accept help if I need it.

And then, somehow, I'll have another cup of tea.

Tea to Go • *A Party in a Basket*

Tea is a portable feast and a wonderful vehicle for sharing. Here's an easily transportable tea party that can go visiting in the home of a friend or climb a mountain to enjoy the view. If you prefer, you can give the whole basket as a gift—with a teacup, a spoon, and all the goodies.

If you take your tea party to the park or to the beach, you will have to carry a portable stove or brew the tea ahead of time, strain it, and carry it in a thermos. Wrap sandwiches well and pack on ice in a small foam cooler or a thermal pack. Everything else will go easily in a large picnic basket, ready to enjoy.

Good-Quality Teabags or Spiced Tea Mix
Cream-Cheese and Chopped-Pecan Sandwiches on Raisin Bread
My Favorite Butter Cookies
Homemade Nut Bread with Three-Apple Apple Butter

SPICED TEA MIX

1 cup dry instant tea (can use decaffeinated)
2 cups dry powdered orange drink
3 cups sugar (may use half sugar substitute)
½ cup hot cinnamon candy
1 teaspoon ground cinnamon
½ teaspoon powdered cloves
1 package (about 1 cup) lemonade mix

Mix all ingredients and place in a covered container. Makes 1½ quarts. To give as a gift, pack in a small jelly jar with lid. Tie a ribbon across the neck with a bright plastic teaspoon. Also, include directions for mixing: one heaping tablespoon to one cup hot water.

MY FAVORITE BUTTER COOKIES

2 sticks unsalted sweet butter (softened)

1 cup sugar
1 egg, separated
1½ tablespoons Amaretto or
½ teaspoon almond extract
2 teaspoons grated orange zest
¼ teaspoon salt
2 cups flour
¾ cups sliced almonds

Preheat oven to 300°. Beat together butter and sugar until light and fluffy (about 3 minutes). Add egg yolk, Amaretto or extract, orange zest, and salt; beat well. Stir in flour and blend well. Spread and pat the dough evenly into a 10 x 15 inch jellyroll pan. Beat egg whites until foamy and brush evenly over the dough. Sprinkle almonds over top. Bake 40 minutes or until light golden brown. Cut into 2-inch squares while still warm.

THREE-APPLE APPLE BUTTER

This spread is delicious with raisin toast or any nut bread.

1 pound unsalted sweet butter
1 Granny Smith apple, quartered with core and skin
1 winesap apple, quartered with core and skin
1 Macoun apple, quartered with core and skin
(You may use any combination of cooking apples, as long as some are tart and some are sweet.)

Place all ingredients in a heavy 4-quart saucepan. Cook 30 minutes over medium to low heat, lowering heat as apples cook and stirring occasionally. Force mixture through a sieve or stainless-steel strainer. Cool, cover saucepan, and refrigerate. Makes 3 cups.

If of thy mortal goods thou art bereft

And from thy slender store

Two loaves alone to thee are left,

Sell one, and with the dole

Buy hyacinths to feed the soul.

PERSIAN POET C. 1300

Fill Me with Beauty

CREATING AND EXPERIENCING LOVELINESS

Tea really isn't necessary to life as we know it.

There are more efficient ways of quenching thirst, of filling our daily nutritional needs.

And it is certainly possible to live life without afternoon teatime (although the entire nation of England might dispute that fact). No doubt there are more productive ways to spend an afternoon than chatting with a friend over a steaming cup of tea.

Yet the spirit of the tea party does touch on something I believe is fully necessary to life as it was meant to be.

The spirit of the tea party is, at least in part, the spirit of beauty. And I am fully convinced that we humans need beauty in order to live rich and fulfilling lives.

People wither when their lives are deprived of beauty.

People grow and flourish when they are able to respond to the beauty around them and create their own forms of beauty.

And the ritual of teatime allows room for both receiving and giving loveliness.

The very act of preparing for tea is an act of creating beauty. There is an art to placing tea cakes just so on a platter, adding the perfect touch of a garnish, arranging fresh flowers in a sparkling crystal vase, and polishing silver until it gleams. There is an art to serving guests, to making them feel comfortable.

I love to arrange a simple tea tray for someone who is a guest in my home—a tiny vase with a single rosebud, a gleaming miniature oil lamp, a pocket-sized book of poems or pictures, and of course an elegant floral teacup and plate.

I also love to host a larger gathering of friends. A shining candlelit buffet table, an elaborate assortment of tea foods, the hum of conversation as guests gather around the fire—all these bring me immense pleasure, and part of the pleasure is knowing I helped put this lovely event together.

Creating beauty in this way is hard work, of course, but that is part of the joy. When I invite my friends to tea and offer them a lovely time, I benefit too, because the work of creating something beautiful enhances the satisfaction of it.

I also find that being involved with making things beautiful increases my sensitivity to the lovely things around me. Or more likely, it is the other way around. How can I possibly create a thing of beauty if I have not first experienced the beautiful?

Beauty is all around us, of course. Our world, with all its sordid problems, still brims with breathtaking loveliness. And one of the benefits of the teatime ritual is that of slowing us down enough to notice what is beautiful around us.

When I sit quietly on our patio in the morning with a cup of tea, I find I am much more acutely aware of the natural beauty around me—the swelling sunrise, the flowers blooming in their boxes by the door, the birds warming up their voices, the smell of blossoms on the breeze.

Even indoors, as I sit quietly to read or just to think, I am more aware of listening and looking and appreciating—more sensitive to beauty and my need for it.

And teatime provides its own beauty as well. A traditional tea is above all a feast of loveliness, a delight to the senses.

Fingers delight in the cool smoothness of bone china, the nourishing warmth of steam rising from a cup, the contrasting textures of linen and lace, the coolness of a wafting breeze.

Nose tingles at the intoxicating mix of yeast and butter and cinnamon and roses—and tea, of course.

Ear is soothed by lovely chamber music or warm conversation or even exuberant birdsong.

Eyes revel in the dainty symmetry of tea sandwiches painstakingly prepared and arranged, of sugar cubes piled artfully in their bowl, of violets and ferns painted delicately on the gleaming teapot. (It must be a delight to be an artist who works in porcelain!)

And all this happens before my tastebuds begin to experience the sweet and savory delights that have been prepared.

Being surrounded by beauty opens little windows that allow our spirits to breathe. Surely we were not meant to be immune to the wonders about us! And surely we have been given the gifts of creativity and sensitivity partly so that we can grow more attuned to beauty, to the way things were meant to be.

My heart still sings when I remember the beauty of that perfect summer day. It was hot, but not too hot for our garden tea party. My friend Toni Sims, whom I had met in Mississippi and come to know over the phone, had just flown out for her first visit to California. And I had planned this tea party so she could meet my family and close friends.

The garden area near our pond was the chosen spot for our tea that day. I felt that little thrill of anticipation as I set out small tables and covered them with white cloths. I carried out my silver tea set, my delicate china plates, and of course my teacups. Toni's husband, Tommy, had sent flowers as a surprise for the special occasion, and we set them in a place of honor.

> *We taste with our eyes as well as our mouths.*
> —*Chef Aaron Patterson*

Dish by dish, the food table was filled—a lovely carrot cake, dainty cucumber sandwiches, tempting chocolate mints and lemon squares, dishes of clotted cream and homemade jam from Great-Grandma Gertie's kitchen. The intoxicating fragrance of raspberry tea floated over it all.

Four generations of the women in our family gathered that day to celebrate Toni's visit. My mother-in-law Gertie Barnes came. So did my daughter Jenny and my "daughter-in-love" Maria and of course my granddaughter Christine. Each brought her dearest friend, so there were nine of us who sat down to tea in our flowing dresses and flower-trimmed bonnets. A lovely soft breeze swept the skirts of our dresses; I felt almost like Scarlett O'Hara serving tea on the grounds!

Hours seemed to vanish as we sat sharing stories and friendship…and a fair amount of carrot cake!

That day gave us all a gift…the gift of beauty. And of course the beauty came from more than cucumbers and clotted cream. More was involved than beautiful clothes and beautiful manners and beautiful food.

> *Whatsoever is lovely…think on these things.*
> —The Book of Philippians

You see, the most beautiful part of any tea party are the faces of friends…the sounds of their voices…the touch of their hands…and the fragrance of friendship mingling with the lovely aroma of the tea.

I really do believe it:

> *The beauty I see*
> *over tea*
> *is thee.*

The Sounds of Teatime

Music provides a beautiful accompaniment to tea, engaging yet another of the senses. Here are some ideas for incorporating music into your teatimes:

• Play the radio. Choose an FM station that plays the kind of music you like with a minimum of talk. Check ahead of time to make sure the station won't be broadcasting the news at the hour you've scheduled the party.

• Play a tape or CD. I prefer strings or classical piano, although any quiet instrumental music will complement the quiet beauty of teatime. (Most classical pieces labeled as "chamber music" will suit beautifully, but do listen ahead of time!) Dance music from the 1930s, when "tea dances" were popular in England, would also be an interesting choice, and quiet jazz or "easy listening" works as well. Vocal music is fine unless the words or music call attention to themselves and distract guests from enjoying one another.

• Hire musicians. For a larger party, live music may be more affordable than you think. Many amateur or student groups would love to play for a minimal fee or simply for the experience, but be sure to audition them ahead of time, and do offer them some tea and appreciation! Try a string quartet, a recorder ensemble, a harpist, a cellist, or a classical guitarist. The music director of a large church, the office of a college music school, or even the high school band or orchestra director may be able to help you locate musicians.

• Play it yourself. If you or your friends are musical, a brief recital or songfest before or after tea can recall the days when people gathered to make their own beautiful entertainment. How about gathering around a piano to sing, or having a talented friend provide a short concert of art songs from the golden age of tea?

If Teacups Could Talk

Tea al Fresco • *A Springtime Garden Tea Party*

A garden tea has to be my favorite type of tea party. I love to set up a pretty table out by our pond or on our patio or even in the tree house, pick a vaseful of beautiful blooms, and set out my most beautiful dishes. Somehow the tea and the food seems to taste twice as wonderful when enjoyed outdoors.

If you live in an area with no yard or garden, take your tea party to the park, or by a river, lake, stream, or beach, or even to the back of a pickup truck along the road. Just find a spot you like and enjoy. (Remember to keep perishable items refrigerated or in an ice chest until just before you serve the tea!)

Raspberry Tea
Egg Salad Sandwiches
Lemon Angel Food Cake
Chocolate Mints
Scones with Mock Devonshire Cream and Gertie's Apricot Jam

RASPBERRY TEA

1 pot freshly brewed tea (any kind you like)
Fresh raspberries—3 to 5 for each cup
Mint leaves and lemon slices (optional)

Brew tea according to the directions in Chapter 1. Before pouring, put fresh raspberries in the bottom of each cup. Allow to sit for a few minutes to let the raspberry flavor permeate the tea. Or if you prefer, pour tea over raspberries in a pitcher and then serve over ice with mint sprigs and lemon slices.

EGG SALAD SANDWICHES

2 hardboiled eggs, chopped fine
½ cup mayonnaise
Salt and pepper to taste
1 teaspoon chives, finely chopped
8 thin slices white or wheat bread
Butter

Mix mayonnaise with eggs, chives, salt, and pepper. Spread each slice of bread with a thin layer of butter. Divide the egg salad among 4 slices of the bread; top with the rest of the bread. Trim the crusts and cut each sandwich into 3 parallel sections to make finger slices. Refrigerate or keep in a cooler until right before serving time.

LEMON ANGEL FOOD CAKE

This looks beautiful and is very quick and easy.

1 prepared angel food cake
3 ounces lemon pudding mix (not instant)
2 cups water
1 lemon for peel
2 tablespoons lemon juice
2½ cups heavy cream
14 ounces flaked coconut

Prepare pudding mix using 2 cups of water. Remove from heat and stir in lemon juice and peel. Pour into medium bowl, cover, and refrigerate one hour. Split cake into five layers. Whip 1 cup cream and fold into lemon filling with 7 ounces coconut. Spread evenly ove r each layer. Cover and refrigerate overnight. Whip remaining cream with ½ cup confectioners' sugar and vanilla. Frost top and sides using coconut for topping.

GERTIE'S APRICOT-RASPBERRY JAM

This recipe is from my husband's mother. Gertie makes the best jams, and this is one of my very favorites. I serve it at teas all the time and always get compliments!

2 pounds apricots (6 cups pared, pitted, and sliced)
¼ cup water
4½ cups sugar
1½ cups raspberries

Add water to apricots. Add sugar and raspberries and cook until jam is desired consistency. Pour into sterilized jars and seal while hot.

*Celebrate the happiness that friends are
always giving, making every day a holiday
and celebrate just living.*

AMANDA BRADLEY

Fill Me with Celebration

A PERFECT EXCUSE FOR A PARTY

When someone says "Let's party!" do you automatically think of tea?

Probably not—but what a shame!

The popular term *partying* tends to conjure up images of loudness and excess, and tea parties certainly don't fit that image. But why should we let a hyped-up, beer-bash view co-opt our ideas of celebration?

Tea parties by nature are quiet, civilized, moderate, defined by tradition. Their only excess lies perhaps in the area of cholesterol (and that too can be moderated). And yet a teatime celebration can be far more satisfying than the rowdiest "blowout."

There is something about a tea party that brings out the best in people—the best behavior, the best intentions, the best attitudes. We expect a little more of each other when we come to tea, and we tend to live up to those expectations. We give a little more. Surely that in itself is cause to celebrate!

In their very quietness, tea parties allow people to draw closer and enjoy each other more. Tea may call for a quieter celebration—but also a more intimate, more meaningful one. You can spend an evening at a loud cocktail party or a crowded reception without making real contact with another human soul. That's hard to do at a tea for teatime requires personal presence.

Teatime celebrations can be festive and joyous, yet at the same time they are gentle on our bodies and spirits. They provide enjoyment without overload—such a tonic for overstressed nervous systems!

But where does the festivity fit in this quiet celebration?

First of all the traditional nature of the tea party says, "This is a special time." In a jeans-and-fast-food culture, the very act of dressing up and gathering around a glistening array of china and silver feels memorable indeed. In fact I would guess that teatime in this informal age feels even more like a celebration than it did in Victorian times.

Yet even while the formality of teatime makes it feel special, the inherent coziness and intimacy of tea makes it warm and comforting and delightful. Teatime celebrations are formal, but they are also welcoming, personal, non-threatening. Somehow sharing tea makes ordinary occasions seem special and special occasions seem comfortably ordinary.

A celebration over tea is also a reflective and deliberate celebration. Tea is not conducive to mindless revelry, but it is very supportive of conscious, deliberate joy. Teatime calls us to think about what it is we're celebrating—the meaning of the occasion and the relationships of the people involved. Over tea, we celebrate personally, with eye contact and conversation.

For any occasion, therefore, tea can add a note of warm, mellow joy. It's a wonderful way to recognize the transition of a graduation or a wedding. It provides a gracious way to honor accomplishments such as a new job or the completion of a project. It adds a special touch to the observance of special days such as Mother's Day or

Secretary's Day. Whatever the occasion, the beautiful rituals of preparing and serving tea give the unmistakable message of "I care."

My friend Dolly Carlson, whose Irish heritage instilled in her a deep appreciation for the joys of tea, used a teatime celebration to mark her daughter's transition to adulthood. This "Sweet Sixteen" tea was not a birthday party for Catherine's peers, but a kind of coming-of-age celebration, an Irish variation on the Jewish Bas Mitzvah. The preparations were elaborate and formal. Whole families—neighbors, church friends, teachers—came to honor and recognize this special transition. The result was a celebration that neither mother nor daughter has ever forgotten.

But the celebration of the teacup is not just for special, one-time-only occasions. Tea also adds a celebratory touch to regular gatherings. Adding a tea party to any get-together tends to change our perspective, to slow us down a bit, to remind us of what we're doing, why it is important, and who are our companions and colleagues in the endeavor. People who meet for business or for pleasure or for mutual support can come to see each other in a new way as they enjoy teatime together.

And of course, tea can be a celebration in itself—an act of appreciation for the little everyday wonders that make up the texture of our lives. Every teatime is a sort of celebration—of the world around us, of each other, of simply being alive. A coffee company may have coined the phrase, but the spirit of the tea party is truly one of celebrating "the moments of our lives."

Tea-party celebrations can be disarmingly simple or impressively elaborate. There's a time for small expressions of joy, and there's also a time to pull out the stops and make teatime unforgettable. For me, the "pull out the stops" time comes every Christmas—the season when I need the teacups' message of celebration most acutely.

You see, I love Christmas, but I find it easy to become bogged down in all it takes to make Christmas Day happen. Every year my tummy tightens up as I consider the work of shopping, wrapping, planning, baking, decorating, inviting—all in addition to my regular duties as a wife, daughter, parent (and grandparent), not to mention my writing and speaking schedule!

I sometimes find myself asking, "Why am I always the one who has to do it all—

make the plans, set the table, do the shopping, wrap the gifts, light the candles, create the traditions? If I don't do it, who will—and will it get done at all? Will the memories be created, the traditions kept?"

It is important to me that the spirit of Christmas is felt, the love is expressed, the memories are passed on—and that's why I choose after all to do all the work involved. But as I tend to all the billions of tasks that are necessary for the season to happen, I need something to help me keep it all in perspective.

My Christmas tea party helps me do that. It warms up our holiday and reminds me of the true purpose for all my preparations.

This is the time when I like to go all out and create a celebration we will all remember. I usually invite a group of women who are close to me, although I have invited men as well. The party is weeks in the preparation, and then the time arrives.

> *Life is a cup to be filled, not drained.*
> —Anonymous

The tea table gleams with snowy linen and pearly china. Fresh-baked cakes and cookies preen proudly on their doily-lined platters. The white candles in their crystal-clear holders cast a golden glow over fragrant pine garlands, red berries, and shiny red apples. Christmas carols beautifully rendered by a symphony orchestra (on CD!) float in the air. My apron of white starched ruffles says, "Welcome! I've prepared this Christmas tea just for you!"

I love to decorate each guest's plate with a little candle held in a special clip—the same kind used many years ago in Europe to secure little candles on the Christmas tree. I clip a candle to each plate. Then we pour the tea, select our goodies, and gather in the decorated "great room" of the converted barn where we live. The cheery warmth of the blazing fireplace sets the tone, and the evergreen smell of the decorated Christmas tree fills the air along with the music. We can almost hear the angels singing!

Now the real celebration begins. I light the candle of the person nearest to me and ask her to share a Christmas thought or Christmas blessing. After she speaks, she then lights the candle of the person next to her, who also shares her Christmas thoughts. Around the room we go, with each person sharing a bit of her heart.

"I love Christmas because…"

"The best Christmas I ever had…"

"The hardest Christmas for me was…"

"Christmas reminds me of…"

"All I want for Christmas is…"

By the time all the plate-candles are lit, we have each given something of ourselves, but have received so much more. Now the candlelight picks up the iridescence of tears on our cheeks. We hear stories of joy—a new grandbaby born, a book completed, a relationship reconciled. And we also hear stories of pain—a miscarriage, a house fire, a child on drugs. My beautiful guests have become as transparent to each other as the warm liquid in their cups. The tissue box moves quickly around the room.

My candle is last to be lit, and my heart is so full that it's hard to speak as I take in the beauty before me—young girls, single women, mothers, grandmothers, even great-grandmothers, all touched by the spirit of the Christmas tea. Our time of celebration together helps us put the holiday season into focus, reminding us all that it is indeed the season of celebration—and that we really do have reason to rejoice.

My friends leave the Christmas tea with their cups of celebration full to overflowing. My cup is full too, and my Christmas has truly begun.

Perhaps that is the true gift of a teatime celebration: It fills our cups with joy and warmth and friendship.

May the echo of the teacups' message be heard not only at Christmas, not only on special occasions, but anytime friends come together:

"Let's have a tea party soon—and celebrate!"

> *My dear, if you could give me a cup of tea to clear my muddle of a head I should better understand your affairs.*
>
> —Charles Dickens

Before We Meet • A Study Group Tea Party

How many meetings do you attend in the course of a week? Most of the people I know are heavily involved in church groups, PTA, discussion forums, civic organizations, or business networks. A simple or elaborate tea party can add a note of celebration to any of these gatherings.

If you are a member of a book study group, for example, why not begin your meeting with a tea party? Gather around the tea table first; perhaps the centerpiece could feature the book chosen for today's discussion. Then, if the setup permits, carry your cups and plates with you so you can sip and nibble while you talk. Brew another pot of tea midway through the meeting and pour another round.

Apple Tea

Almond Chicken Tea Sandwiches

Shortcake Biscuits with Clotted Cream

Sliced Fruit

APPLE TEA

Any kind of herbal tea or mellow
　　black tea such as Darjeeling or
　　English breakfast
Clear apple juice
Sugar to taste
Cinnamon sticks

Brew tea using boiling apple juice instead of water. Use 1 teaspoon tea or 1 teabag per cup of juice. Pour tea into cups. Sweeten with sugar and stir with a cinnamon stick.

ALMOND CHICKEN TEA SANDWICHES

3 boneless, skinless chicken breasts,
　　cooked and chopped coarsely
½ cup slivered, blanched almonds
½ cup mayonnaise
White or wheat bread

Mix chicken, almonds, and mayonnaise. Butter well each slice of bread. On half the slices, spoon about 3 tablespoons of almond chicken mixture. Top with remaining slices. Stack three sandwiches tall. Wrap in wax paper and again in a slightly dampened kitchen towel. Let filling set for at least an hour. Unwrap, cut off crusts, and cut into triangles. For a different look, cut sandwiches in 2-inch strips and set on a doily sideways, with the strips of chicken filling showing.

SHORTCAKE BISCUITS

This delicious recipe comes from Colleyville, Texas.

2 cups all-purpose flour
1½ tablespoons sugar
1 tablespoon baking powder
1½ teaspoon salt
¼ cup unsalted sweet butter, cut into 1½-teaspoon-sized pieces and frozen
1½ cup plus 1 tablespoon heavy cream
1 egg yolk
1½ teaspoon vanilla
2 tablespoons confectioners' sugar

Preheat oven to 375°. Mix together flour, sugar, baking powder, and salt. Add butter and blend in quickly, just until the butter is broken into pieces about the size of small peas. Add 1 cup of the cream and combine with a fork until moistened. Immediately turn out dough onto a lightly floured board and knead about ten times. (You want small lumps of the butter to be visible.) Roll out to a thickness of ¾ inch, trying to keep the dough in a square shape. Cut into 6 squares and transfer to an ungreased cookie sheet. Mix the egg yolk with the remaining tablespoon of cream and brush on biscuits. Then make a cream glaze by whipping the remaining 1½ cup of cream, vanilla, and 1½ tablespoons confectioners' sugar. Brush this over the yolk glaze. Sprinkle with the remaining confectioners' sugar and bake 15 to 20 minutes, until golden brown. Serve with fresh fruit or very good jam, clotted cream, or crème fraîche.

Teacups in the Office • A Healthy Tea Break at Work

If you work in an office, your colleagues and coworkers probably make up an important part of your world. After all, you see these people more hours of the day than you probably see your family! Every day you share the excitement and the stress of the busy workplace environment. Why not set aside a special afternoon to share a cup of tea together?

Every office is different, of course, so the specific arrangements for an office tea will have to reflect your particular setting. Perhaps you will want to invite members of your department to the conference room to celebrate a birthday. Or you can make everybody's day by setting up a tea service in the lunchroom and treating employees to a warming cup as they come for their breaks. There are many ways to accomplish your purpose of injecting a little loveliness into a busy workday.

If you want to include the entire office, why not make simple invitations to send via interoffice mail—or even E-mail?

Tea is a meal for all seasons; it's also suitable for all occasions.

—Angela Hynes

If you will be serving many people, you may want to use pretty paper cups or perhaps even cups and saucers from a rental service. But why not ask your coworkers to bring cups from home? You'll have the fun of seeing what everyone brings, and the varied patterns will add a nice homey touch to your office tea.

Make your serving table as pretty as possible—cloth, flowers, candles, and tea service. One woman I know went to a fabric store and pieced together a simple lace tablecloth to fit the huge conference-room table. That lace cloth became a staple for office parties for years afterward.

This is one setting where the convenience of teabags may be welcome. I find that most people love herbal infusions such as cinnamon apple or almond, and if you use this kind of tea you won't need to provide milk.

Depending on your arrangements, you might need to make your tea at a different place from where you serve it, and you might need several teapots. Tea cozies—little "blankets" to keep the pot warm—can serve you well in such a situation.

It goes without saying, of course, that you should clear your arrangements with your supervisor and with anyone else whose work might be affected. And unless you are serving tea as part of an official office function, you will want to make arrangements not to interrupt the workday for too long.

The menu for this office tea is simple and easy to transport, and health-conscious office workers will appreciate its low calories and wholesome ingredients.

MRS. B's WHOLE-WHEAT CARROT CAKE

2 cups whole-wheat flour (or use all-purpose flour for a lighter consistency)
1 tablespoon toasted wheat germ
1 teaspoon baking powder
1 teaspoon baking soda
1 teaspoon salt
1 teaspoon ground cinnamon
1¼ cups honey
¼ cup brown sugar
1½ cup unsalted sweet butter (melted)
1 teaspoon molasses
1 teaspoon vanilla
4 eggs
3 cups finely shredded carrots (easiest in a food processor)
1 cup chopped pecans or walnuts

Preheat oven to 350°. Grease and flour two 8-inch or 9-inch round baking pans. In mixer bowl combine flour, wheat germ, baking powder, baking soda, salt, and cinnamon. Add honey, sugar, butter, molasses, and vanilla; beat on low speed until combined. Add eggs one at a time, beating well after each egg, then stir in carrots and nuts. Pour batter into pans and bake 30 to 35 minutes, or until toothpick comes out clean. Cool on wire racks for 10 minutes, then remove from pans and cool completely before spreading with cream-cheese frosting. (You can also make in a bundt pan.

When it is cool, dust with powdered sugar.) Serve in thin slices.

CREAM-CHEESE FROSTING FOR MRS. B'S CARROT CAKE

8 ounces cream cheese, softened (use a "lite" version if desired)
1½ cup unsalted sweet butter
2 cups sifted confectioners' sugar
One teaspoon vanilla
1½ teaspoon honey or molasses
¼ cup chopped pecans (optional)

In a mixer bowl, beat together cream cheese and butter until very fluffy. Then beat in remaining ingredients. Chill to spreading consistency.

SWEET LEMON SCONES

2 cups all-purpose flour
½ teaspoon salt
4 tablespoons sugar
1 tablespoon baking powder
3½ tablespoons butter
1 8-ounce carton lowfat lemon yogurt
2 eggs, separated
1 teaspoon grated lemon peel
3 tablespoon heavy cream

Preheat the oven to 425°. Stir together flour, salt, sugar, and baking powder. Using a pastry blender, cut butter into flour mixture until it resembles coarse crumbs. Stir together the lemon yogurt, egg yolks, and lemon peel. Add to the flour mixture and stir lightly with a fork. Add cream 1 table-

spoon at a time until dough begins to clump together. Gather dough on lightly floured surface and knead just three or four times or until the dough holds together. (Do not overwork!) Pat dough into a rectangle about ¾ inch thick and cut with 2-inch round cookie cutter. Place scones on ungreased cookie sheet and brush tops with beaten egg whites. Bake for 10 minutes or until light brown. Serve warm. Makes approximately 16 scones.

The scones can be frozen before baking. Place on cookie sheet in freezer until firm, then put into plastic bag and keep frozen until ready to bake. Add just a few extra minutes to the baking time.

YOGURT CHEESE

This is a nice lowfat alternative to clotted cream—tangy and refreshing with sweets. Or you can add herbs or minced vegetables and use it as a spread for crackers and vegetables.

2½ to 3 cups plain or vanilla yogurt, set without gelatin, gums, or starch (check label)

Line a colander with a double thickness of cheesecloth and place colander in a bowl. Put yogurt into colander and cover with plastic wrap. Refrigerate overnight. The liquid will drain from the yogurt, leaving smooth solids. Throw away liquid and add seasonings, if you wish, to the remaining yogurt cheese. Makes 1 cup.

She was passionately interested in everything I did. She spoke with candor and good grace. Then, defying the reality of crutches and straightened knee, on wings of hospitality, she flew to brew the tea.

—TOM HEGG, *A CUP OF CHRISTMAS TEA*

If Teacups Could Talk

A Cup of Christmas • A Special Holiday Tea

Christmas is a special time for friends and family to gather together, and a Christmas tea offers a wonderful chance to celebrate your relationships and the season itself. Let your Cup of Christmas tea be your special holiday gift to your friends, your family, and yourself.

Start early to plan your tea so you can approach your celebration with serenity instead of panic. (I always begin planning in October for a mid-December tea.) Find beautiful Christmas-themed note cards with no message inside to use for invitations. And have fun when it comes to planning the decor and the menu, the Christmas season offers so many wonderful possibilities. Take full advantage of all the wonderful decorating materials that are available—sparkling red-and-green fabrics, lush and fragrant greens, all kinds of candles. Load your table with a groaning variety of sweet and savory foods. And let your holiday message be one of abundant good cheer and memories in the making.

Almost any "Christmas party" food lends itself to tea-party fare. I like to take advantage of rich flavors and wonderful ingredients.

Spiced Russian Tea
Southern Pecan Cake
Fresh Blackberries or Other Fruit
Marscarpone or Brie
Assorted Christmas Cookies

End your time together by singing carols around the fire or reading aloud from a Christmas classic—O'Henry's *The Gift of the Magi*, for example, or Tom Hegg's *A Cup of Christmas Tea*. The Christmas story from the Gospel of Luke is the perfect way to put the whole season in perspective!

SPICED RUSSIAN TEA

Russian tea was originally imported to Russia from China by camel caravan and traditionally served from a samovar or large tea urn. Russians drink their tea with lots of lemon and sugar, but no milk.

6 teaspoons Russian blend or any good black tea
1 pinch cloves
1½ pints freshly boiled water

Place tea and cloves in pot, add water, and brew for five minutes before pouring. Add sugar and lemon to taste.

SOUTHERN PECAN CAKE

This wonderful flourless cake was served at a Christmas tea in the home of Susan Vineyard of Portland, Oregon. Everyone loved it!

2 cups pecans (very fresh)
5 large eggs, separated
⅔ cup sugar
1 teaspoon vanilla or 1 tablespoon cognac

Preheat oven to 325° and grease and flour an 8-inch springform pan. Roughly chop 1½ cup pecans; set aside. Finely chop the remaining pecans; add to other nuts. (A food processor makes the chopping process much easier.) Beat the egg yolks in a large bowl until they are lightly fluffed, add sugar and beat hard until the mixture turns a lighter shade of yellow and is smooth. Gently fold in nuts with a rubber spatula, add vanilla or cognac and mix well. Beat egg whites until stiff but not dry. With a rubber spatula gently fold a third of the egg whites into the nut mixture to lighten it, then fold in the remaining egg whites. Spoon batter into prepared pan; it should be no more than ¾ full. Place the pan on the middle shelf of the oven and bake 50 to 60 minutes, or until cake springs back when lightly touched. Cool in pan for 5 minutes, then run a thin knife around the sides to loosen the cake. Unclamp the pan and let cake cool completely before removing it from the bottom of the pan. Coat top and sides with Dark Sweet Chocolate Frosting. Makes 6 to 8 servings.

DARK SWEET CHOCOLATE FROSTING

8 ounces dark sweet chocolate (Tobber's, Lindt, or Callebout)
1 cup heavy cream

Break chocolate into coarse pieces and melt in double boiler over barely simmering water. Add cream and stir until smooth. Remove the pan from heat and beat hard. Place in the refrigerator to firm up (about 30 minutes). Frost cake in a swirl design.

If you are cold, tea will warm you;

if you are too heated, it will cool you;

if you are depressed, it will cheer you;

if you are exhausted, it will calm you.

WILLIAM GLADSTONE

Fill Me with Imagination

A COLLECTION OF TEA PARTY IDEAS

If teacups could talk, they would say so much—about the past, and also about the future. But surely their strongest message would be: "Use me—and use your imagination."

Teatime offers so many wonderful possibilities for nurturing friendships—this book has touched on just a few. I invite you to make full use of your creativity as you make the spirit of the tea party part of your life.

To give you some ideas, here is a gathering of tea-party possibilities:

Send a birthday tea party in a box. I received one of these with everything I needed to celebrate: a wonderful Mississippi mud cake, napkins, tablecloth, box of teabags, artificial flowers, and a book of poems. What a wonderful way to lift someone's spirits on a special day!

Share midnight tea with your loved one. After a full day spent traveling to seminars—or just a busy day at home—Bob and I often sit down and unwind over a cup of herbal tea or just hot water and lemon.

༔ Think tea whenever you give a gift. For a housewarming, a canister of good tea or a tea cozy are thoughtful offerings. For birthdays or special occasions, a lovely English teacup is a memorable present. Each Christmas my girls (daughter, daughter-in-law, granddaughter) receive another part of their tea-party collection: a white starched tablecloth or apron, lace-edged napkins, a crystal candleholder, a silver spoon or butter knife, or a new teacup to add to their collection.

༔ Enclose a teabag with your teatime invitations. Add a note inviting guests to enjoy one tea now and one tea later.

༔ When serving a basket of scones or tea breads, sprinkle oatmeal and /or granola around the basket to create a smile of surprise.

༔ Look for lovely old linens, trays, vases, cups, teapots, or spoons at garage sales or antique stores.

༔ For a homey tea, set your tea table with an old or new quilt. The centerpiece could be an old hat from Grandma's trunk or a pretty bonnet. Have guests bring family photos to share.

༔ Invite a friend to come for tea and bring along an unfinished craft project. After you enjoy your tea, play some soothing music, do your project, and talk.

༔ For a sweet but different cup of tea, try adding a tablespoon of maple syrup to your cup. This would be a wonderful touch for an autumn tea—with decorations of colored leaves and bright apples.

༔ It's fun to prepare your own tea goodies, but there's nothing wrong with buying them. Try a bakery, a deli, or a tea shop for delicious edibles. Then put your effort and imagination into setting a beautiful table and enjoying your teatime companions.

༔ Enliven almost any tea gathering by having each guest bring his or her teacup. You will learn so much about each other as you talk about your cups. Some will be from wedding sets, some family heirlooms, some hastily purchased for the occasion.

༔ Write out your teatime invitations on a doily and send in a pretty pink envelope.

༔ Ask your tea guests to wear a hat, old or new.

༔ After a nap on a lazy afternoon, surprise your mate with a tea tray in bed.

◠ Ask each tea guest to bring a yard of wallpaper—a remnant or a sample. When guests arrive for tea, have each one cut out her own placemat—heart-shaped, oval, scalloped, square, rectangular, or whatever she fancies.

◠ To make your own chocolate tea leaves for garnish, simply brush melted chocolate onto a real leaf. Let harden and gently remove the leaf.

◠ Formal afternoon teas call for white linen, but for other occasions make your own tea cloth and serviettes from lovely cotton fabric or sheets—just cut and hem. Make your tea cloth 45 or 54 inches square and hem the napkins into 12-inch squares.

◠ Let your guests stir their tea with cinnamon sticks placed by the sides of their cups.

◠ Address the envelopes for your Christmas cards in August over a glass of iced tea with lemon.

◠ Have a rose-petal tea. Ask guests to wear a rose (or give them one from your garden) and decorate your table with a vase of roses. Scatter rose petals over your tea tray. Collect your rose petals and shake with cinnamon oil in a zippered plastic bag to make a lovely potpourri. Did you know you can also make tea from rose petals? Brew 2 cups of black tea and mix in a large bowl with 1½ cups dried rose petals (unsprayed), ¾ cup lemon verbena leaves, and 2 tablespoons dried lemon peel. Strain. Strong light will affect the delicate taste of this tea, so keep it out of the sunlight.

◠ Host an "adopt a grandma" or "adopt a kid" tea. Have everyone bring a guest who is over sixty—or under eight. This could be a great party for teenagers.

◠ Enjoy a lavender and lace tea on a summer afternoon. Ask guests to wear lavender or lace and decorate your table appropriately. You can even scent whipped cream by pouring the cream over lavender blossoms, letting it sit overnight, and then whipping. Use in a fruit salad or serve with scones.

◠ Have tea in the moonlight out on the lawn—a perfect occasion for a tea-basket picnic. Or pack your basket and take to the beach to enjoy the sunset.

◠ For a bridal shower, prepare a lovely tea table with shining white cloth and white and silver centerpiece. Ask guests to bring tea things as gifts—teacups, little spoons, linens— or pool your gift money and buy the teapot that matches the bride's china selection.

Borrow an idea from elementary school and have a "show and tell" tea. Each guest brings a special item to share with the other guests. A variation on this could be a collection tea; guests bring one item out of whatever they collect.

An ethnic tea can be wonderful fun. Plan your tea around the traditions of some of the other great tea-drinking nations besides England—including China, Japan, Israel, India, Russia, Scotland, Holland, or Ireland. Another idea would be to ask guests to bring an item (or wear a costume) that reflects their own national heritage.

Gather a group of special friends and go as a group to visit a local tea room or an inn that specializes in afternoon tea. This would be a wonderful reunion tradition: Gather each year at the tea room of your choice and reflect on the past year together.

Mary Mac's TeaTimes Newsletter is a wonderful source of teatime lore, creative ideas, wonderful recipes, and information about hard-to-find items. For information contact: Mary Mac's TeaTimes Newsletter, P.O. Box 841, Langley WA 98260.

Build your tea around your favorite book that features tea. Some wonderful possibilities: *Alice in Wonderland, Anne of Green Gables, Winnie the Pooh, Little Women.*

A TEATIME BLESSING

·

*Lord, grant that our time together
be steeped in serenity, sweetened by sharing,
and surrounded by the
warm fragrance of your love.*

AMEN

If Teacups Could Talk